*World Food*

# THAILAND

JUDY WILLIAMS

# *World Food*
# THAILAND

*p*

This is a Parragon Book

This edition published in 2005

Parragon

Queen Street House

4 Queen Street

Bath BA1 1 HE, UK

Created and produced by The Bridgewater Book Company Ltd.

*Project Editor* Stephanie Horner

*Project Designer* Michael Whitehead

*Photography* David Jordan

*Home Economist* Judy Williams

*Location photography* Kim Sayer, Simon Punter

ISBN: 1-40545-707-4

Printed in China

NOTES FOR THE READER

• This book uses both metric and imperial measurements. Follow the same
units of measurement throughout; do not mix metric and imperial.

• All spoon measurements are level: teaspoons are assumed to be 5 ml, and
tablespoons are assumed to be 15 ml.

• Unless otherwise stated, milk is assumed to be full fat, eggs and individual
vegetables such as potatoes are medium, and pepper is freshly ground
black pepper.

• Recipes using raw or very lightly cooked eggs should be avoided by infants,
the elderly, pregnant women, convalescents, and anyone suffering from
an illness.

• The times given are an approximate guide only. Preparation times differ
according to the techniques used by different people and the cooking times
may also vary from those given.

# contents

# INTRODUCTION

10 Welcome to Thailand or, rather, to a taste of it in your own home. Much as we would all like to go there, it's not always possible, so this is a taste of what it would be like, but without the long flight. In this Thailand, you have to do the cooking yourself; but don't worry, Thai cuisine is easy to tackle, the results are stunning and the taste is wonderfully distinctive. You'll master the basics easily and soon be able to impress your friends and family.

The main problem used to be finding the ingredients, but with everyone travelling, reading and eating out more we have all become increasingly ambitious and experimental in our cooking. Consequently, smaller more specialist stores as well as supermarkets have had to meet this need, and our shops are now full of lemon grass, chillies, galangal and coconut milk. Although most ingredients are readily available, we have offered an alternative for the things that are trickier to find, such as palm sugar and Thai basil (see pages 32–3).

Having been largely unexplored by Westerners for much of its past, Thailand is now one of the most popular places to visit and, with that interest, comes a fascination for the food. Set between China and India, the flavours and tastes of those two countries have had an influence on Thai food, especially as the first settlers are thought to have come from southern China. It was they who introduced the techniques of stir-frying and steaming that have now become vital parts of Thai cooking.

Until 1939, Thailand was called Siam. Its ancient capital was Sukhothai, meaning 'dawn of happiness' in Sanskrit. The country has seen many battles, and frequent changes of rulers, each bringing their own forms of government, language and religion. Under the influential eye of King Ramkhamhaeng, the fabulously beautiful curly Thai alphabet was designed,

Buddhist art was created and the cuisine and culture developed. Ayuthaya became a new capital, superseding Sukhothai in the mid-14th century and, after two hundred years of fighting and change, it was, in turn, destroyed. Its replacement, Thonburi, was founded as a royal capital in 1782 on the site that is now Bangkok.

## Regional cuisine

Thailand is bordered by Malaysia, Myanmar (formerly Burma), Laos and Cambodia. The flat central plains that lead to the Chao Phraya estuary are ideal for rice growing, much of which is exported. The northeast of the country is made up of the drier Khorat plateau which slopes up to the mountains that include Doi Inthanon, the highest peak in Thailand. The east coastline runs for 1,500 km/930 miles from Trat province to the Malaysian border along the Gulf of Thailand. The west coastline down the peninsula runs 560 km/348 miles along the Andaman Sea from Rahong to Satun, past Phuket, a very popular holiday destination. There are also a great number of islands dotted along the coast.

There are three main seasons. The warmest period is from March to May. June to October is the rainy

*Thailand is a place of distinct seasons, with June heralding a time of humidity and heavy rains.*

season, when it pours for a while each day, leaving a warm and humid atmosphere. The coolest time is from November to February. During these months the mountainous north gets much colder.

Obviously the varying topography, soils and climate combine to determine which crops can be grown in the different regions and, although certain recipes are traditional wherever you are in Thailand, there may be subtle, local twists of flavours and ingredients. The country appears to divide into four main areas, each of which has its own particular style of cooking and eating.

The north of Thailand is full of interesting ruins and temples. This region was on the route from the East to the West taken by some of the earliest trading travellers. It was the most easily conquered part, adapting and changing when wars and battles took place. It is also the region that, allegedly, produces most of the country's opium.

The people of the north use more steamed, sticky and glutinous rice and their curries are generally thinner in texture, as coconut milk is not used in their cooking. The influences of Myanmar and Laos can be seen in some of the curry dishes. Buffalo and pork are the main meats and I have heard that buffalo placenta is a highly desirable treat!

The northeast is the poorest and most infertile of Thailand's four regions. Droughts and other natural disasters have had an effect on its regional dishes. Ingredients such as meat and coconut are replaced with delicacies including grasshoppers, snails and ants' eggs. Cooks have obviously had to be creative and inventive because the local produce is far less abundant but, as the country has developed, they are

Left *Hot chillies grow widely in Thailand's poorer north-east, and consequently feature heavily in the local dishes*

Overleaf *Bankok's floating market*

better able to source more interesting and useful ingredients. However, rice, the staple of Thai cuisine, has been growing in this part of the country since 4000 BC, when China was still growing and eating millet. Luckily, there are plenty of chillies grown in this part of Thailand – the locals like their food hot and consequently use a lot of them.

Southern Thailand is a long peninsula and has the advantage of the dense, central rainforest and lush climate as well as two coastlines. There are plenty of palm plantations, so coconut milk and palm sugar feature in many of the dishes. The proximity of the sea means an abundance of fish and shellfish, from prawns and scallops to squid and lobster, so many local recipes include these ingredients. They also produce crops of cashew nuts, pineapple and other fruits, such as pomelo.

The flat central plains are packed with vegetable gardens, paddy fields and orchards, which, in turn, means that local produce is of high quality and incredibly plentiful. Most of the rice eaten in Thailand is grown here with more than half the country's revenue coming from its export. There are many ceremonies connected with the planting, growing and harvesting of rice in appreciation of it, especially around Songkran – the Thai New Year. This occurs in mid-April, lasts for three days and marks the sun's moving from Aries into Taurus. Lots of water is thrown around during this celebration to symbolize cleansing and renewal. Buddha is cleaned as a mark of respect and as a blessing from the older people to the younger generation. Plenty of fun is had at the same time.

Abundant rice and the variety of fresh fruit and vegetables mean a wide assortment of dishes are prepared. The four large cities in Thailand, including Bangkok, are situated in this area, so there are huge numbers of people to cater for and feed.

One way most Western visitors get their taste

and knowledge of Thai food is from the throngs of specialist street stalls in the main cities. Hawkers have their own portable small stalls in which they carry around their tools, ingredients and means of cooking. Bangkok also has a floating market, with long, thin boats, packed with fresh or cooked foods. Entire families can be seen travelling in these boats, crouching on the bottom or perched on sacks, while the cooking is done over a small charcoal or gas burner.

For many young people packing their rucksacks and trekking off around the world today, Thailand seems to be the place to start. The Khao San Road in Bangkok is often the backpacker's first stop for a taste of real Thai food for very little outlay. Traditionally, hawkers sold freshly cooked noodles,

*The flat central plains are packed with vegetable gardens, paddy fields and orchards ... local produce is of high quality and incredibly plentiful*

but their repertoire may now include bowls of steaming soup, barbecued meats, sticky rice and banana crêpes – perfect for hungry travellers and city workers alike. The hustle and bustle of these street markets is very much a way of life for the huge crush of people who live and work in the large cities. However, away from these large tourist attractions, Thai people stick to a more traditional diet. Cooking for visitors is very different from the everyday meals that are eaten at home. Few Thai people use recipe books. They have learned by watching their families cook and it is very much a 'cook, taste and add a little more' style of cooking.

# *Chinese foodstores ... are filled with ingredients that we're often barely able to recognize, let alone know how to cook*

## Buying and storing

Until recently, fridges were not common in Thailand and consequently, many Thai people shop daily. Shopping is usually done in the morning and the food is cooked the same day. However, all the usual, sensible rules about cooking, storing food, chilling and freezing still apply to Thai cooking. As Westerners are more likely to shop weekly, we need to ensure that the ingredients we use are the best on the day of purchase if we're not going to eat the food for 3–4 days. Use only fresh produce and keep it chilled until required. Check the 'best-before' and 'use-by' date stamps and be extra careful when buying fish and shellfish, as these should be eaten on the day of purchase or frozen immediately – but only if they haven't been frozen before.

Some Thai dishes, such as vegetable curries, can be prepared the day before if they are slightly under-cooked, cooled and then stored in the fridge. This gives the seasonings a chance to develop and mature, so the final curry will have a greater depth of flavour, and the vegetables do not fall apart or become too soggy to taste good when reheated.

For the same reasons, you may also want to undercook slightly a meal that you intend to freeze. Freezing also degrades flavour and texture, so again vegetables will be softer and blander. Meat dishes, especially chicken, however, must be thoroughly cooked prior to chilling or freezing. Make sure the dish is cold, pack it into a freezerproof container or bag, date and label it clearly and freeze for no longer than three months. Don't forget that food should

never be frozen for a second time. Rice, on the other hand, is best eaten on the day of cooking. Leftover rice can be kept in the fridge overnight but discarded if not used the next day. Chill food only once it is cold and cover dishes with clingfilm. The aromas may penetrate everything else in the fridge and who wants to drink milk or orange juice when it has a tang of chillies and coriander!

## Sourcing ingredients

Large supermarkets stock a range of sauces, noodles, dried mushrooms, chilli sauces, curry pastes, coconut milk and many of the herbs and spices needed for Thai cooking. There will always be a few things that are hard to find and specialist Chinese foodstores are often the place to hunt down these items. These shops are filled with ingredients that we're often barely able to recognize, let alone know how to cook, and they also have a strange, exotic smell. Asking what foods are, how to prepare them and then experimenting with them are great ways of getting to know Thai food. Nevertheless, with a simple recipe to follow and the determination to succeed, you will soon get to grips with the art of Thai cooking.

## Equipment

You need at least three good chopping boards, one for meat, one for vegetables and herbs, and a third for fish. Scrub them clean before and after use, especially meat and fish boards. Most people use plastic, which is dishwasher-safe and can be sterilized, rather than wood or marble for fish and meat.

Knives need to be varied in size – large blades for chopping herbs and slicing meat and fish, small ones for preparing vegetables.

*Left Kaffir limes yield little juice but are very full flavoured*

*Overleaf Many agricultural tasks are carried out manually*

*The most important piece of equipment is the wok. All types of food – curries and soups, stir-fries and noodles – may be cooked in it*

Above and opposite *Paying their respects to images of Buddha is part of daily life for the majority of Thai people*

Overleaf *River plains provide the most fertile farming soil*

A pestle and mortar is traditional, but many cooks prefer the easier, faster option of a food processor, with a blender and a small grinder for chopping, grinding and puréeing ingredients, processing fish for fish cakes, and making curry pastes.

Probably the most important piece of equipment is the wok. All types of food – curries and soups, stir-fries and noodles – may be cooked in it. It is routinely used for deep-frying in Thailand. You can buy a two-handled wok, but I prefer the version with one wooden handle: it doesn't get so hot.

The traditional steel wok needs seasoning before use as it is sold with a protective oiled coating to prevent it from rusting. Scrub off the coating in warm soapy water, rinse well and half dry. Stand the damp wok on a hob over a low heat until it is dry. Drizzle a little oil into the wok and wipe it around the inside with a piece of kitchen paper. Continue heating gently until the oil smokes and burns off, then repeat with another coating of oil. The wok will darken in colour and should never be scrubbed again, just wiped carefully. If food sticks or burns and the wok does need scrubbing, it will probably need to be seasoned again. All steel woks are sold with the manufacturer's instructions, so read through before using for the first time.

Non-stick woks are also available, usually from supermarkets and department stores. These won't rust, don't need oiling and can be washed up like other saucepans. Check if they are dishwasher-safe.

Other tools include the usual assortment of spatulas, slotted spoons, measuring jug and spoons, a vegetable peeler, a garlic press, a whisk and so on. You also need a steamer for dumplings and spring rolls. Bamboo steamers, placed over a wok of

# As a rule, Thais eat three meals a day and at least two of those will include rice

simmering water, are favoured by both Thai and Chinese cooks. If you opt to use a metal steamer or colander, it needs to be flat-based, rather than one with sloping sides. This type is great for draining and steaming small quantities of vegetables, but you need a flat base on which to arrange small parcels of food so that they cook evenly. Ensure the steamer fits tightly over the wok or saucepan of simmering water or most of the steam will escape around the edges.

A useful tool that is fun to learn to use is the cleaver. It looks unbelievably heavy and awkward, but once you get used to the weight and the fact that it's very sharp, it is an amazingly versatile piece of equipment – excellent for cutting thicker pieces of meat, as well as finely chopping onions or garlic. That will really make you feel like a proper Thai chef.

## Thai meals

As a rule, Thais eat three meals a day and at least two of those will include rice. Breakfast might be some sort of rice-based soup and city-workers might stop for noodles at lunchtime from one of the street hawkers. A traditional dinner, maybe in the company of guests, will be the main meal of the day. Several curries will be cooked and served, perhaps with a salad and some vegetable dishes. This main Thai meal will also be accompanied by rice. Thai people are not worried about eating food hot – it is often served either warm or at room temperature. They eat mainly with a spoon and fork, not chopsticks, using the fork to load the spoon, although chopsticks are more popular when eating noodles. Dessert may be one of a delicious range using such ingredients as mung bean flour and fruit to make cakes, or coconut milk with sliced fruit to make jellies.

## Preparation

So, now that we have a better understanding of Thai food, let's get on with cooking some of the fabulous, varied ingredients that identify the cuisine. Thai-style cooking is now very popular in the West because it is so quick, but you do need to spend time beforehand on preparation.

Do read the recipe thoroughly and have all the ingredients ready. Prepare and chop all the chillies, ginger, vegetables etc. Ensure you have Thai fish sauce to hand and enough oil to deep-fry those prawns. Do check the method too, as it's a nuisance to find you should have peeled the tomatoes before adding them to the dish and there they are, pristine, whole, with their skins firmly on. (*For reference: use a sharp knife to mark a cross on the base of each tomato, place in a bowl and cover with boiling water. Leave for 5 minutes, rinse under cold water and peel off the skins. Quarter, deseed and chop the flesh.*) I do give weights of vegetables but you will know how much you and/or your family will eat and can adjust quantities accordingly. Everything should be flexible, so if in doubt about the heat of a curry paste, add half the quantity, cook and taste. Equally, if you are only cooking for two, halve the quantities; for more than four, increase them accordingly. Be creative in how you use the recipes – but do be sure to stick to either metric or imperial measurements.

Eating Thai food is an amazing experience because the flavours are such a marvellous mixture of hot, sweet and sour. The taste is astringent, leaving your teeth feeling clean and your mouth alive. In most people's opinion, chilli is the key ingredient in Thai cooking. It is used in most savoury recipes, freshly chopped or blended into a paste. Yet the secret is less about heat, rather the harmony derived from the delicate taste and fragrance of coconut milk, lemon grass, galangal, kaffir lime leaves, palm sugar and Thai fish sauce – the quintessential elements of Thai food. So, on with the recipes and, please, relax and enjoy the experience. Cooking is meant to be fun and this book is certainly about just that.

## Noodles

Rice is Thailand's main staple, but noodles run it a close second and, in some ways, noodle dishes typify the very essence of Thai cuisine. Variety – in flavour and texture – is the keynote and noodle dishes are almost infinitely diverse. Noodles may be combined with any number of other ingredients, including meat, poultry, fish, seafood, vegetables and the ubiquitous chilli. They are served hot or cold, in soups and salads, deep-fried or stir-fried, braised or shaped into attractive little nests. A noodle dish may be one of several different dishes – all of equal importance – served as part of a family meal. Equally, a steaming bowl of freshly cooked noodles tossed in a flavoursome sauce makes a welcome mid-morning snack or a tasty treat bought from a roadside stall late in the evening.

The versatility of noodle dishes is further extended by the wide variety of types available. Rice noodles, which range in thickness from thin strands to flat ribbons, are the most popular. Fried with seafood, tofu, vegetables and a selection of sauces, they could be described as Thailand's national dish. Dried rice noodles are sold in bundles and are usually soaked in warm water as a preliminary to further cooking. You will find fresh rice noodles in specialist stores and some supermarkets. Egg noodles,

*The busy, colourful markets are the place to buy the freshest spices, fruits and vegetables that provide the keynote flavours to Thailand's cooking*

*Noodles may be combined with any number of other ingredients ... meat, poultry, fish, seafood, vegetables*

familiar from Chinese cooking, are also widely used in Thailand. These are made from wheat flour, egg and water and come in a variety of shapes and sizes. Usually they are cooked in boiling water and may then be added to soups or stir-fries towards the end of cooking. Boiled and very thoroughly drained, they can also be fried to make crisp noodle cakes.

Cellophane noodles, also known as bean thread, glass or transparent noodles, are made from ground mung beans. They must be soaked to soften them and can then be added to stir-fries, curries and they are a favourite for salads. Rice vermicelli are very thin, rather brittle noodles, usually sold in somewhat unwieldy bundles. Once soaked, they cook almost instantly in water, stock or coconut milk. They can also be deep-fried, creating wonderful tangled nests. Crisp-fried rice vermicelli, combined with pork, prawns and vegetables and tossed in a piquant sweet-and-sour sauce, is a popular special-occasion dish known as *mee krob*.

Noodles are not hard to cook, but timing is critical as they can quickly become sodden and unappetizing. Check the packet instructions for the recommended cooking time. Take especial care when precooking noodles before stir-frying, deep-frying or adding to soups. Remove them from the heat as soon as they are just tender, drain thoroughly and then refresh under cold running water to prevent further cooking. Drain well again, particularly if they are to be fried.

Dried noodles may be kept for months in an air-tight container. Keep fresh noodles for several days in the refrigerator but do check the 'use-by' date.

## Rice

Every Thai person probably eats about 500 g/1 lb 2 oz of rice a day, whether in the form of noodles or as plain rice, for breakfast, lunch or dinner. It certainly seems to be the main staple, owing much to the fact that no wheat grows in Thailand. The Thais also use rice flour, which has a very distinctive texture, to thicken their sauces and curries, sometimes to dust meat that is to be stir-fried or to bind meat and other ingredients together.

A large bowl of rice forms the centrepiece on a Thai family table, surrounded with vegetable, fish, meat and other curry dishes. The Thais never serve rice as an accompaniment to a main dish.

Rice dishes, as well as noodles, can easily be bought from the hawkers and various vendors that fill the streets in cities such as Bangkok and Chiengmai. Popular dishes include coconut rice, egg-fried rice and hot, spicy rice.

There are two main types of rice in Thailand. In the north and northeast, a sticky, glutinous, short-grain variety is preferred, often eaten with the fingers. Because of its texture, the rice can be rolled into balls and then dipped into sweet or savoury sauces and condiments. Glutinous rice is usually soaked before steaming. You should not rinse it more than twice, otherwise you will wash off all the starch that makes it sticky.

The second type of rice, a long-grain variety, is the fluffy, fragrant rice, such as jasmine and basmati, which is often more popular in the Western world than the glutinous. Fragrant rice can be boiled or steamed and then sometimes fried. It is important that you don't overcook rice, or it will become stodgy and bland. There should always be twice as much water as rice. The easiest way to tell whether it is cooked is to bite a grain between your front teeth. Alternatively, press a grain between your finger and thumb: it should break into three pieces.

Remember to experiment with your rice dishes; this is, after all, what Thai cookery in this book is all about. Use a mix-and-match method and devise your own creations by combining different flavourings. Try throwing a couple of lime leaves, some chilli, grated coconut or a lemon grass stalk in with the rice while it is cooking – just remember to take out the leaves or lemon grass before you serve it.

Rice is also used for desserts and sweets. Short-grain rice can be turned into a special Spicy Rice Pudding (see page 240) for a sweet and spicy Thai treat. To make rice crackers Thai cooks deliberately leave a crisp layer of rice on the base of the saucepan in which it has been cooked, then remove it and put it in the sun to dry. The crisp pieces are fried in hot oil and dipped in syrup or coconut.

## Cooking rice

People are often worried about cooking rice, thinking that it always sticks and goes clumpy, but this is only when it is overcooked. Check the packet instructions and follow them for perfect rice every time.

Sticky, glutinous rice needs to be soaked overnight and then steamed for 8-10 minutes, until tender. It can then be eaten hot or packed into a container, levelled off and chilled. The resulting slab can be cut into small square rice cakes that are often served with satay dishes.

There are several different ways of cooking jasmine or other long-grain rice and opinions differ as to which is best. The first way is to put the rice into a measuring jug, up to the level of 115 ml/4 fl oz per person. Wash it and then tip into a saucepan. Measure double the volume of water and pour it into the saucepan. Bring to the boil, lower the heat, cover and simmer very gently for 12–15 minutes, without stirring or disturbing it. Turn off the heat and leave, covered, for 3–4 minutes before serving. A second method is to put the rinsed rice into a saucepan and add water to cover it by about 2.5 cm/1 inch, or the distance to the first knuckle on your index finger. Add a pinch of salt, cover, bring to the boil and simmer for 1-2 minutes, then turn off the heat and leave in the saucepan, covered, for 25 minutes. The water should have been absorbed; the rice should be fluffy and ready to eat.

Other people prefer the easy option and use the boil-in-the-bag variety. But cooking ordinary rice isn't tricky at all and once you have found the method that suits you, rice will be on the menu more often.

## Curry pastes

We've all eyed up the colourful rows of curry pastes lining the shelves in the supermarkets, ready-made for our convenience, and do use them if you want to: there's nothing wrong with that. The authentic ones save time and effort chopping what seems like hundreds of chillies, and all the clearing and washing up. However, it is more fun to have a go yourself. It also means the flavours will be fresher and taste cleaner and stronger, and, without doubt, home-made curry pastes beat the bottled versions hands down. Do use good-quality, fresh ingredients, as the final product will last longer and taste better.

There are several types of curry paste and although the basic ingredients are similar, they all add a different flavour and degree of heat to the recipe. It is also helpful to understand how they vary and why, and at least you'll know whether to pick a yellow, red or green curry next time you're dining in a Thai restaurant. Thai green curry is the hottest. This is because the Green Curry Paste calls for small, hot fresh green chillies, not dried ones. Red Curry Paste

*Overleaf Tending the all-important paddy fields in the country's great central plains is back-breaking work for Thailand's rice farmers*

*There are several types of curry paste, and, although the basic ingredients are similar, they all add a different flavour and degree of heat to the recipe*

is milder, as it usually uses dried red chillies, and Yellow Curry Paste (see page 93) is the mildest. There is also a Penang Curry Paste (page 114), which has a Malaysian influence, and the famous Mussaman Curry Paste (page 124) is a favourite with Thai Muslims and is much more like an Indian flavouring.

So, get out your chopping board and sharp knives, and rubber gloves for preparing the chillies, unless, like me, you use a sharp knife and fork to avoid handling them. You'll need a blender, food processor, a grinder or pestle and mortar to make pastes, and a wok or large frying pan.

---

*curry paste recipes*

*Green Curry Paste*

1 tbsp coriander seeds

1 tbsp cumin seeds

1 tsp shrimp paste

15 fresh green bird's eye chillies, chopped

2 shallots, chopped

6 garlic cloves, chopped

2.5-cm/1-inch piece of fresh galangal, chopped

2 lemon grass stalks (white part only), chopped

6 kaffir lime leaves, chopped

2 tbsp chopped coriander root

grated rind of 1 lime

1 tsp salt

1 tsp black peppercorns

*Red Curry Paste*

1 tbsp coriander seeds

1 tbsp cumin seeds

2 tsp shrimp paste

12 dried or fresh red chillies, chopped

2 shallots, chopped

8 garlic cloves, chopped

2.5-cm/1-inch piece of fresh galangal, chopped

2 lemon grass stalks (white part only), chopped

4 kaffir lime leaves, chopped

2 tbsp chopped coriander root

grated rind of 1 lime

1 tsp black peppercorns

Dry-fry the coriander and cumin seeds in a heavy-based frying pan, stirring constantly, for 2–3 minutes, until browned. Remove from the heat and grind to a powder with a pestle and mortar or spice grinder or process in a blender.

Wrap the shrimp paste in a piece of foil and grill or dry-fry for 2–3 minutes, turning once or twice. Put the ground spices, shrimp paste and chillies into a blender or food processor and process until finely chopped. Add the remaining ingredients and process again to a smooth paste, scraping down the sides as necessary.

---

*A variety of delicious fruits and vegetables are bundled together and sold as snacks outside the temples of Thailand*

# In the Thai kitchen

**Beansprouts** These are usually sprouted mung beans, but many other beans can be sprouted. They need to be used quickly, as they soon deteriorate. Added at the last minute, they give crunch and a nutty flavour.

**Cardamom** These small, hard seeds are sold in the pod and used whole to add a spicy taste to stocks, curries, even ice cream. Ground seeds are used in curry pastes.

**Chillies** The most-used chillies are red or green – the orange and yellow ones only represent different stages of ripeness. Large smooth chillies are usually milder. Longer, thinner, knobbly ones are hotter and the very small bird's eye chillies are fiery hot. Cutting out most of the membrane with the seeds removes a lot of the heat but not the flavour. Use rubber gloves to protect your fingers and don't rub your eyes! The leaves are often used as a vegetable; hot or sweet **chilli sauces** served as an accompaniment.

**Chinese dried mushrooms** Assorted dried mushrooms are now more widely available in the West. They need soaking in hot water before use. The stalks on larger, whole mushrooms are tough and should be discarded. The soaking water is often added to the dish as well, but may need to be diluted as it can be very strong.

**Chinese leaves or Peking cabbage** is a long, pale, densely packed vegetable with frilly leaves. Shred it and add towards the end of cooking time so that it remains crunchy, or use in salads. It is also sold pickled and canned, for use as a side dish.

**Chinese or garlic chives** are longer and flatter than Western ones, often sold with their flowers attached. Use them chopped or whole as a garnish, or steamed whole for 1–2 minutes for tying tiny food parcels.

**Choy sum or Chinese flowering cabbage** has long stems and leaves with pretty yellow flowers. Use in the same way as **Broccoli** – both are full of goodness – especially in stir-fries. Don't overcook: it turns grey and soggy, loses its vitamins, and tastes horrible.

**Coconut** Probably the best-known ingredient in Thai cooking. Canned coconut milk (buy the unsweetened) is usually half solid and half liquid. Creamed coconut comes in solid blocks. Desiccated coconut needs reconstituting with hot water. To make a thick creamy coconut sauce, use 85 g/3 oz desiccated coconut to 200 ml/7 fl oz water. For a thinner sauce, mix 55 g/2 oz desiccated coconut with 250 ml/9 fl oz hot water.

**Coriander** Fresh coriander is an essential ingredient in Thai cuisine. The roots are used in sauces or marinades; the leaves chopped and stirred into sauces during cooking or sprinkled as a garnish and a flavouring.

**Cumin** These seeds can be added to hot oil to flavour it before cooking begins. They are also dry-fried in curry paste recipes. Whole seeds and ground cumin are easily found in supermarkets and foodstores.

**Curry pastes and sauces** Thai curries are thinner and more fragrant than Indian ones. Home-made curry pastes take time to make; prepared pastes are quick and easy, and usually come marked with degrees of heat. Always add them gradually, especially if you don't like your food too spicy. Ready-made curry sauces are less concentrated than the pastes. For an instant meal, pour them over noodles or toss in rice.

**Fish sauce** Made from small fish and shrimp that have been fermented in the sun, this salty, thin, brown sauce is an essential part of Thai cooking. Most recipes – and not only fish ones – include it in small quantities (the flavour is very intense).

**Galangal** Similar in taste to ginger but subtler in flavour. Used in soups, curries and spice pastes. The fresh peeled root can be sliced or grated; in its dried form galangal must be soaked to reconstitute. Galangal is also sold grated or sliced in jars.

**Garlic** Used in almost all savoury Thai recipes, usually added at the beginning, often stir-fried with onion.

**Ginger** Peppery-hot and refreshing, ginger plays a major part in Thai cooking. A fresh root is pink – blue or grey edges indicate that it is stale and too fibrous.

**Lemon grass** The tough stalks of this grass are snapped into pieces and added to soups or stocks. For curry pastes, only the finely chopped inner white part is used. The stalks can be frozen and used as required.

**Limes and lime leaves** Although common limes can be used, smaller kaffir limes are more familiar in Thailand. The thick rind is full of flavour but there is almost no juice. They can be eaten if chopped small, but discard them if using whole. The leaves add an astringent flavour to stocks, soups and curries.

**Long beans or snake beans** Stringless beans which add little flavour, but crunch to curries and stir-fries.

**Magic paste** Using the trinity of Thai ingredients: a whole bulb of garlic, peeled and ground with a bunch of fresh coriander leaves and roots and 55 g/2 oz white peppercorns. Keep in the refrigerator for 3–4 days or freeze in small amounts. It is also sold in jars.

**Oils** Most cooking in Thailand uses palm oil, as it is in plentiful supply and flavourless. You can use sunflower or vegetable oil, but olive oil cannot be heated to stir-frying temperature and is too strong. Sesame oil may be used sparingly, more for flavour, or in marinades.

**Palm sugar** Derived from the flower of the palm tree. It varies in colour and is less sweet than cane or beet sugar. It comes in a block that can be crumbled or melted. Use soft, light brown sugar as an alternative.

**Rice flour** A fine white flour used to thicken soups and bind meaty mixtures. Cornflour is a substitute.

**Shrimp paste** A thick paste with a very strong smell made from dried salted shrimp. Use in small amounts, as its flavour is very intense. It must be cooked before using but doesn't need to be stored in the refrigerator once opened. Tiny salted **dried shrimp** may be found in Chinese foodstores. They need to be ground or processed and are then added to pastes and sauces.

**Spring roll wrappers** These square pastry wrappers come ready for use in packs of about 20. Leftover sheets can be frozen for another time. Handle them carefully. Keep covered with a damp tea towel or clingfilm until ready to use, as they dry out quickly.

**Thai basil or holy basil** leaves are thinner and flimsier than the more familiar basil used in Italian cooking. Thai basil has a mild aniseed flavour, a lovely smell and adds a fantastic flavour to curries and soups, but substitute common basil if you can't get the Thai one.

**Tofu** Made from solid beancurd – highly nutritious and incredibly versatile as it readily absorbs flavours. The most useful is the firm white tofu that comes packed in its own liquid. Use it as it is or, far tastier, cut into cubes, deep-fry and add to curries and stir-fries. Ready-fried tofu is also sold.

**Wonton wrappers** Square pastry sheets, rather like small spring roll wrappers, are made from wheat flour and egg. They can be steamed for a softer parcel and deep-fried for a crispy one.

STARTERS

Thai people don't really eat starters. Small portions of each dish – rice, curries and salads – are served on plates or in bowls and eaten together, either with a spoon and fork or just with the fingers. However, in the West meals are generally separated into courses, so we have to adjust the recipes here to suit this custom.

Among the selection of recipes here to be served as starters you will find there are quite a lot of finger foods, which are served warm, and should be picked up, dunked into a tasty dip and eaten immediately. There are other dishes that might need a spoon and fork, as they are quite soupy or involve eating rice or noodles.

The wok really is a most useful piece of equipment. Because it is deep as well as wide, it can be used for cooking everything, whether it is stir-fried vegetables with tofu or deep-fried wontons. Alternatively, if you don't possess one, you will need a large frying pan or heavy-based saucepan for these recipes. These do need to be large ones, as you will need plenty of room to toss food, mix and stir-fry vegetables or brown pieces of meat or fish. (You also could use a deep-fat fryer, but do make sure the oil is clear, light and clean. Once it has turned dark, it should be changed. This is important as it will affect the flavour of, say, spring rolls if the last thing you cooked in your fryer was battered fish.)

Deep-fried food can be very greasy. Probably all of us have bitten into a spring roll only to have hot oil pour out, burn our chins and spoil our clothes, so take care to put all fried foods on kitchen paper and pat well with more kitchen paper to remove as much of the oil as possible. An off-putting greasy texture and taste will also overpower the delicate flavour of the filling in a deep-fried parcel, whether

wonton or spring roll, or a crispy battered prawn. If the oil is still fairly new and clean, but full of bits of batter or seeds, you can filter it. Allow the oil to cool completely first. Line a sieve with a double layer of kitchen paper and stand over a deep bowl. Gradually pour the cold oil into the sieve – it won't all fit at once – and filter it through the paper and into the bowl below. Discard the kitchen paper and its contents and pour the oil back into the frying pan or wok. You may be able to do this twice but after that the oil will need changing; as it gets darker and darker it will affect the flavour of the food.

Some dishes need to be cooked in batches, so put the cooked batch into a warm oven or under a hot grill while you cook the next batch, or simply cover

## *Starters are a way of stimulating the appetite rather than satisfying it. Your guests should be left feeling they could eat that all over again*

with foil and keep on top of the oven. Since most of these starters are cooked quite quickly in hot oil, they don't cool down very fast. In any case, if you adopt the Thai style of eating, food is usually served lukewarm, rather than hot. Serve small portions because, although they may not look much, remember there are two more courses to follow. Starters are a way of stimulating the appetite rather than satisfying it. Your guests should be left feeling they could eat that all over again and knowing that there is even better to come.

Whatever you choose, remember that the job of the starter is to set the taste buds alight for the next course.

# corn fritters
## *khao ped chup pang*

**SERVES 4**

*for the fritters*

3 spring onions, chopped finely

325 g/11½ oz canned sweetcorn kernels, drained

1 red pepper, deseeded and finely chopped

small handful of fresh coriander, chopped

2 garlic cloves, crushed

2 eggs

2 tsp caster sugar

1 tbsp fish sauce

2 tbsp rice flour or cornflour

vegetable or groundnut oil, for shallow-frying

*for the dip*

2 red peppers, deseeded and halved

2 tomatoes, peeled, deseeded and chopped coarsely

1 tbsp vegetable or groundnut oil, for shallow-frying

1 onion, chopped

1 tbsp Red Curry Paste (see page 31)

3–4 sprigs fresh coriander, chopped

1 Combine all ingredients for the fritters in a bowl. Heat the oil in a frying pan and fry spoonfuls of the mixture, in batches, until golden brown on the underside. Flip over with a spatula to cook the second side. Remove from the frying pan, drain on kitchen paper and keep warm.

2 To make the dip, put the red peppers on a baking sheet and place, skin side up, under a hot grill, until blackened. Using tongs, transfer to a plastic bag, tie the top and leave to cool slightly.

3 When the peppers are cool enough to handle, peel off the skins and chop the flesh. Put into a blender or food processor with the tomatoes and process until smooth.

4 Heat the oil in a heavy-based saucepan and cook the onion and curry paste for 3–4 minutes, until softened. Add the pepper and tomato purée and cook gently until tender and hot. Stir in the chopped coriander, cook for 1 minute, and serve hot with the fritters.

# wontons
## *kaeow*

SERVES 4

*for the filling*

2 tbsp vegetable or groundnut oil

6 spring onions, chopped

125 g/4$^{1}$/$_{2}$ oz mushrooms, chopped

55 g/2 oz fine French beans, chopped

55 g/2 oz sweetcorn kernels, drained if canned

1 egg, beaten

3 tbsp Thai soy sauce

1 tbsp palm sugar or soft, light brown sugar

$^{1}$/$_{2}$ tsp salt

*for the wontons*

24 wonton wrappers

1 egg, beaten

vegetable or groundnut oil, for deep-frying

plum or chilli sauce, to serve

1 To make the filling, heat the oil in a preheated wok and stir-fry the spring onions, mushrooms and beans for 1–2 minutes, until softened. Add the sweetcorn, stir well to mix and then push the vegetables to the side. Pour in the egg. Stir until lightly set before incorporating the vegetables and adding the soy sauce, sugar and salt. Remove the wok from the heat.

2 Place the wonton wrappers in a pile on a work surface. Put a teaspoonful of the filling in the centre of the top wrapper. Brush the edges with beaten egg and fold in half diagonally to make a small triangular parcel. Repeat with the remaining wrappers and filling.

3 Heat the oil for deep-frying in a wok or large frying pan. Add the parcels, in batches, and deep-fry for 3–4 minutes, until golden brown. Remove from the wok with a slotted spoon and drain on kitchen paper. Keep warm while you cook the remaining wontons. Serve hot with plum or chilli sauce.

40
# crisp sesame prawns
*khung ob gha tord khob*

**SERVES 4**

115 g/4 oz self-raising flour

3 tbsp sesame seeds, toasted or dry-fried

1 tsp Red Curry Paste (see page 31)

1 tbsp fish sauce

150 ml/¼ pint water

vegetable or groundnut oil, for deep-frying

20 large uncooked prawns, peeled with tails intact

chilli sauce, for dipping

1 Combine the flour and sesame seeds in a bowl. Stir the curry paste, fish sauce and water together in a jug until mixed. Gradually pour the liquid into the flour, stirring constantly, to make a thick batter.

2 Heat the oil for deep-frying in a wok or large frying pan. Holding the prawns by their tails, dip them into the batter, one at a time, then carefully drop into the hot oil. Cook for 2–3 minutes, until crisp and brown. Drain on kitchen paper and serve immediately with chilli sauce.

1 Put the eggs, water and Thai soy sauce in a bowl. Set aside. Mix together the spring onions and chopped chilli to form a paste.

2 Heat half the oil in a 20-cm/8-inch frying pan and pour in half the egg mixture. Tilt to coat the base of the frying pan evenly and cook until set. Lift out and set aside. Heat the remaining oil and make a second omelette in the same way.

3 Spread the spring onion, chilli paste and curry paste in a thin layer over each omelette and sprinkle the coriander on top. Roll up tightly. Cut each one in half and then cut each piece on the diagonal in half again. Serve immediately, while still warm.

# omelette rolls

41

## *kai yud sai*

SERVES 4

4 large eggs

2 tbsp water

1 tbsp Thai soy sauce

6 spring onions, chopped finely

1 fresh red chilli, deseeded and chopped finely

1 tbsp vegetable or groundnut oil

1 tbsp Green Curry Paste (see page 31)

bunch of fresh coriander, chopped

42

# fish cakes
## *thot man pla*

**SERVES 4**

450 g/1 lb white fish fillets, skinned and cut into cubes

1 egg white

2 kaffir lime leaves, torn coarsely

1 tbsp Green Curry Paste (see page 31)

55 g/2 oz French beans, chopped finely

1 fresh red chilli, deseeded and chopped finely

bunch of fresh coriander, chopped

vegetable or groundnut oil for frying

1 fresh green chilli, deseeded and sliced, to serve

*for the dipping sauce*

115 g/4 oz caster sugar

50 ml/2 fl oz white wine vinegar

1 small carrot, cut into thin batons

5-cm/2-inch piece cucumber, peeled, deseeded and cut
   into thin batons

1 Put the fish into a food processor with the egg white, lime leaves and curry paste and process until smooth. Scrape the mixture into a bowl and stir in the French beans, red chilli and coriander.

2 With dampened hands, shape the mixture into small patties, about 5 cm/2 inches across. Place them on a large plate in a single layer and chill for 30 minutes.

3 Meanwhile, make the dipping sauce. Put the sugar in a saucepan with 1½ tablespoons water and the vinegar and heat gently, stirring until the sugar has dissolved. Add the carrot and cucumber, then remove from the heat and leave to cool.

4 Heat the oil in a frying pan and fry the fish cakes, in batches, until golden brown on both sides. Drain on kitchen paper and keep warm while you cook the remaining batches. If you like, reheat the dipping sauce. Serve the fish cakes immediately with warm or cold dipping sauce, topped with chilli slices.

*Thai architecture is as colourful and distinctive as the country's cuisine*

*These taste great cooked under the grill, but using the barbecue adds that extra smoky flavour.*

# chicken satay
## *satay gai*

**SERVES 4**

2 tbsp vegetable or groundnut oil

1 tbsp sesame oil

juice of $1/2$ lime

2 skinned, boned chicken breasts, cut into
    small cubes

*for the dip*

2 tbsp vegetable or groundnut oil

1 small onion, chopped finely

1 small fresh green chilli, deseeded and chopped

1 garlic clove, chopped finely

125 ml/4 fl oz crunchy peanut butter

6–8 tbsp water

juice of $1/2$ lime

1 Combine both the oils and the lime juice in a non-metallic dish. Add the chicken cubes, cover with clingfilm and chill for 1 hour.

2 To make the dip, heat the oil in a frying pan and fry the onion, chilli and garlic over a low heat, stirring occasionally, for about 5 minutes, until just softened. Add the peanut butter, water and lime juice and simmer gently, stirring constantly, until the peanut butter has softened enough to make a dip – you may need to add extra water to make a thinner consistency.

3 Meanwhile, drain the chicken cubes and thread them on to 8–12 wooden skewers.* Put under a hot grill or on a barbecue, turning frequently, for about 10 minutes, until cooked and browned. Serve hot with the warm dip.

*cook's tip
Soak wooden skewers in cold water for 45 minutes before threading the meat to help stop them burning during cooking.

*Sculpture and intricate decoration are key elements of Thai art*

46 # beef stir-fry
## *pahd nuea*

1 Heat the oil in a wok or large frying pan and stir-fry the onions, garlic and ginger for 1 minute. Add the beef strips and fry over a high heat until browned all over. Add the vegetables and the two pastes and cook for 2–3 minutes until blended and cooked.

2 Stir in the coriander and basil and serve immediately with rice.

**SERVES 4**

2 tbsp vegetable or groundnut oil

2 medium red onions, sliced thinly

2 garlic cloves, chopped

2.5-cm/1-inch piece root ginger, cut into matchsticks

2 x 115 g/4 oz beef fillets, sliced thinly

1 green pepper, deseeded and sliced

150 g/5¹/₂ oz canned bamboo shoots

115 g/4 oz beansprouts

2 tbsp Magic Paste (see page 33)

1 tbsp Red Curry Paste (see page 31)

handful of fresh coriander, chopped

few sprigs Thai basil

boiled rice, to serve

*Overleaf Any visitor to Thailand will be struck by the imposing gold statues of Buddha*

# 50 crispy spring rolls
*po pia thot*

**SERVES 4**

2 tbsp vegetable or groundnut oil

6 spring onions, cut into 5-cm/2-inch lengths

1 fresh green chilli, deseeded and chopped

1 carrot, cut into thin batons

1 courgette, cut into thin batons

$1/2$ red pepper, deseeded and thinly sliced

115 g/4 oz beansprouts

115 g/4 oz canned bamboo shoots, drained and rinsed

3 tbsp Thai soy sauce

1–2 tbsp chilli sauce

8 spring roll wrappers

vegetable or groundnut oil, for deep-frying

1 Heat the oil in a wok and stir-fry the spring onions and chilli for 30 seconds. Add the carrot, courgette and red pepper and stir-fry for 1 minute more. Remove the wok from heat and stir in the beansprouts, bamboo shoots, soy sauce and chilli sauce. Taste and add more soy sauce or chilli sauce if necessary.

2 Place a spring roll wrapper on a work surface and spoon some of the vegetable mixture diagonally across the centre. Roll one corner over the filling and flip the sides of the wrapper over the top, to enclose the filling. Continue to roll up to make an enclosed parcel. Repeat with the remaining wrappers and filling to make 8 spring rolls.

3 Heat the oil for deep-frying in a wok or large frying pan. Deep-fry the spring rolls, 3–4 at a time, until crisp and golden brown. Remove with a slotted spoon, drain on kitchen paper while you cook the remainder, then serve immediately.

# crispy wrapped prawns

*khung hau tord khob*

**SERVES 4**

16 large unpeeled cooked prawns

juice of 1 lime

4 tbsp chilli sauce

16 wonton wrappers

vegetable or groundnut oil, for deep-frying

plum sauce, to serve

1 Remove the heads and peel the prawns, but leave the tails intact. Place them in a non-metallic bowl, add the lime juice and toss lightly to coat. Set aside in a cool place for 30 minutes.

2 Spread a little chilli sauce over a wonton wrapper. Place a prawn diagonally across it, leaving the tail protruding. Fold the bottom corner of the wrapper over the prawn, fold the next corner up over the head and then roll the prawn up in the wrapper, so that the body is encased, but the tail is exposed. Repeat with the remaining wrappers, chilli sauce and prawns.

3 Heat the oil in a wok or frying pan and deep-fry the prawns, in batches, until crisp and browned. Serve hot with plum sauce for dipping.

52 # crab parcels
*pue hao*

**SERVES 4**

350 g/12 oz canned white crab meat, drained

1 fresh red chilli, deseeded and chopped

4 spring onions, sliced finely

1 tbsp Red Curry Paste (see page 31)

juice of 1/2 lime

1/2 tsp salt

20 wonton wrappers

oil for frying

*for the dip*

50 g/2 oz caster sugar

2 tbsp water

2 tbsp rice wine vinegar

3 pieces stem ginger, sliced

1 tbsp ginger syrup from the jar

1 Put the crab meat into a bowl and add the chilli, onions and curry paste. Stir together with the lime juice and salt.

2 Put the wrappers in a pile and put 1 portion of the crab meat in the middle of the top wrapper. Brush the edges with a little water and roll up the edges to make a small cigar-shaped parcel. Continue to make parcels with the wrappers – you need at least 20.

3 Heat the oil in a wok or large frying pan and fry the parcels, a few at a time, until golden brown. Drain on kitchen paper.

4 Put all the ingredients for the dip in a small saucepan and heat gently until the sugar has melted. Serve warm with the crab parcels.

*Rickshaws are commonly used to travel short distances in Thailand*

## 54 lettuce wraps
*puk hao*

*Make sure you have a plentiful supply of napkins
ready when serving these tasty little parcels.*

**SERVES 4**

1 iceberg lettuce

1 tbsp vegetable or groundnut oil

1 onion, chopped finely

1 fresh red chilli, deseeded and chopped

350 g/12 oz minced pork

200 g/7 oz canned water chestnuts, drained, rinsed
  and chopped

3–4 tbsp Thai soy sauce

1 tsp palm sugar or soft, light brown sugar

1–2 tbsp Green Curry Paste (see page 31)

3–4 fresh Thai basil leaves, torn coarsely

1 Separate the lettuce leaves, wash well in cold water*
  and shake dry. Place all the leaves upside down on a
large plate and chill for 2 hours.

2 Heat the oil in a wok and stir-fry the onion and
  chilli for 30 seconds. Add the minced pork and stir-
fry for 8–10 minutes, until browned and crisp. Stir in
the water chestnuts, soy sauce, sugar, curry paste and
basil leaves and cook for a further 2–3 minutes.

3 Transfer the pork mixture to a warmed serving
  dish and serve immediately with the chilled lettuce
leaves. Each guest can put a spoonful of the pork
mixture into the centre of a lettuce leaf, roll it up
and eat with their hands.

*\*cook's tip*
To separate the lettuce leaves, cut off the stalk and hold
the lettuce under cold running water. As the water runs
between the leaves the weight of it separates them
without tearing.

## steamed spring rolls
### *po pia nuag*

**SERVES 4**

12 rice flour pancakes

12–24 fresh Thai basil leaves

2 tbsp chilli sauce, plus extra for serving

24 cooked peeled tiger prawns

4 spring onions, cut into thin strips

1 carrot, cut into thin batons

55 g/2 oz rice vermicelli noodles, cooked and drained

1 Place the pancakes between 2 dampened tea towels and leave for 2 minutes, until soft. Alternatively, soak them in warm water and lift out one at a time to work on.

2 Place 1–2 basil leaves in the centre of a pancake and top with a little chilli sauce. Arrange 2 prawns on top and then some of the spring onions and carrot. Add a few noodles and roll up. Flip one edge of the pancake over the filling, fold the sides over to enclose it and roll up. Repeat with the remaining pancakes and filling.

3 Arrange the filled pancakes in a single layer in the top of a steamer. Cook over simmering water for 4–5 minutes, until heated through. Serve immediately with extra chilli sauce for dipping.

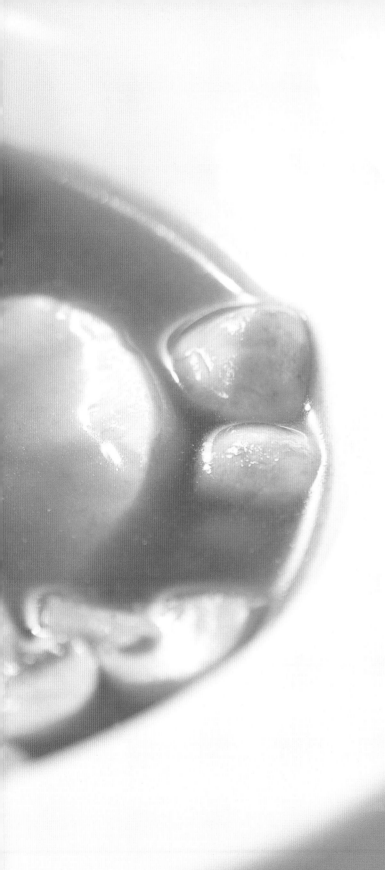

SOUPS

Soups form a major part of any Thai meal and are served at the same time as all the other dishes. In the West, we think of them as an alternative to a starter, maybe a lunchtime snack, or plan to serve a really chunky soup as a main meal. Some soups can be very filling indeed, so you need to plan your menu carefully.

*stir in herbs at the end, so they wilt and flavour the soup as they are gently incorporated into the liquid*

A thin, watery soup with a few mushrooms and a little shredded chicken is definitely one to be served as a starter soup, designed to stimulate the taste buds and wake up the whole mouth ready for the second course. Other soups, such as Prawn Laksa (see page 63), are thickened with coconut milk and contain noodles and so may be enough to satisfy a hungry person looking for a filling lunch.

Cooks in the West may be used to following the basic method for making soup of heating a little oil, lightly sautéing a mixture of vegetables and then adding stock, herbs and seasonings. Thai soups, on the other hand, are often made with heated stock or coconut milk to which vegetables, meat or fish are then added, so no frying is involved. This chapter includes recipes using both techniques. Some of them are made with a combination of Eastern and Western culinary styles and flavourings, while others are more traditional, but there is sure to be something for everyone.

Some of the recipes require stock as a base and, obviously, it is better if you can make your own. However, for the occasions when you don't have the time or inclination, a good-quality stock cube will still give perfectly good results. Those soups that are based on coconut milk, not stock, will be thicker, richer and more filling. Cans of coconut milk are readily available from most large foodstores, as well as specialist supermarkets. Shake the can vigorously

before opening it, or stir well once the lid is opened to incorporate the thinner, watery milk with the coconut cream – you need both.

Although soups are made in a wok in Thailand, you can use a saucepan. Choose one with a heavy base, if possible, especially for the thicker soups, to prevent the liquid from sticking and burning. Most soups are made with 850 ml–1.2 litres/ 1½–2 pints of liquid, but, before you start, check that your saucepan is large enough to accommodate all the ingredients – vegetables, meat or fish and the liquid – and allow room for stirring as well. Cut your root vegetables to a similar size and they will cook in the same time; stir in herbs at the end so that they wilt and flavour the soup as they are gently incorporated into the liquid.

## The wonderful aroma of the flavourings used in Thai soup is enough to make your mouth water

If you are adding rice and noodles to a soup, take care to make sure that when you put them in they will have the correct amount of time to cook. They continue to swell in the hot liquid and both will lose shape and texture if cooked for too long. Once again, do check the packet instructions carefully for perfect results.

The wonderful aroma of the flavourings used in Thai soups is enough to make your mouth water. Once you have found the flavours you like best, you can start experimenting yourself. Some of the soups here are so thin that the stock is transparent, but others, containing rice and eggs, are really thick and very filling. So have fun and play around with the wonderful Thai flavours that make each soup a treat to eat.

# hot-and-sour soup
## *tom yam*

**SERVES 4**

6 dried shiitake mushrooms

115 g/4 oz rice vermicelli noodles

4 small fresh green chillies, deseeded and chopped

6 tbsp rice wine vinegar

850 ml/1<sup>1</sup>/2 pints vegetable stock

2 lemon grass stalks, snapped in half

115 g/4 oz canned water chestnuts, drained, rinsed
    and halved

6 tbsp Thai soy sauce

juice of 1 lime

1 tbsp palm sugar or soft, light brown sugar

3 spring onions, chopped, to garnish

1 Place the dried mushrooms in a bowl and pour in enough hot water to cover. Set aside to soak for 1 hour. Place the noodles in another bowl and pour in enough hot water to cover. Set aside to soak for 10 minutes. Combine the chillies and rice wine vinegar in a third bowl and set aside.

2 Drain the mushrooms and noodles. Bring the stock to the boil in a large saucepan. Add the mushrooms, noodles, lemon grass, water chestnuts, soy sauce, lime juice and sugar and bring to the boil.

3 Stir in the chilli and vinegar mixture and cook for 1–2 minutes. Remove and discard the lemon grass. Ladle the soup into warmed bowls and serve hot, garnished with the spring onions.

*Any visitor to Thailand will return with vivid impressions of the fabulously carved buildings*

# prawn laksa
*khung*

**SERVES 4**

400 g/14 oz canned coconut milk

300 ml/$^1$/$_2$ pint vegetable stock

50 g/1$^3$/$_4$ oz vermicelli rice noodles

1 red pepper, deseeded and cut into strips

225 g/8 oz canned bamboo shoots, drained and rinsed

5-cm/2-inch piece fresh root ginger, sliced thinly

3 spring onions, chopped

1 tbsp Red Curry Paste (see page 31)

2 tbsp fish sauce

1 tsp palm sugar or soft, light brown sugar

6 sprigs fresh Thai basil

12 unpeeled cooked prawns

1 Pour the coconut milk and stock into a saucepan and bring slowly to the boil. Add the remaining ingredients, except the prawns, and simmer gently for 4–5 minutes, until the noodles are cooked.

2 Add the prawns and simmer for a further 1-2 minutes, until heated through. Ladle the soup into small warmed bowls*, sharing the prawns equally among them, and serve.

*cook's tip
Serve the soup immediately, as the noodles will continue to swell and soak up all the liquid. It tastes so fantastic you won't be able to wait anyway.

*Thailand's long coastline means plentiful seafood daily*

64 # sweetcorn and crab soup
*tom jood pu sai khow pod*

**SERVES 4**

2 tbsp vegetable or groundnut oil

4 garlic cloves, chopped finely

5 shallots, chopped finely

2 lemon grass stalks, chopped finely

2.5-cm/1-inch piece fresh root ginger, chopped finely

1 litre/1¾ pints chicken stock

400 g/14 oz canned coconut milk

225 g/8 oz frozen sweetcorn kernels

350 g/12 oz canned crab meat, drained and shredded

2 tbsp fish sauce

juice of 1 lime

1 tsp palm sugar or soft, light brown sugar

bunch of fresh coriander, chopped, to garnish

1 Heat the oil in a large frying pan and fry the garlic, shallots, lemon grass and ginger over a low heat, stirring occasionally, for 2–3 minutes, until softened. Add the stock and coconut milk and bring to the boil. Add the sweetcorn, lower the heat and simmer gently for 3–4 minutes.

2 Add the crab meat, fish sauce, lime juice and sugar and simmer gently for 1 minute. Ladle into warmed bowls, garnish with the chopped coriander and serve immediately.

*Intricate detailing is a feature
of Thai architecture everywhere*

# 66 clear soup with mushrooms and chicken
*tom jood gai sai hed*

**SERVES 4**

25 g/1 oz dried ceps or other mushrooms

1 litre/1³/4 pints water

2 tbsp vegetable or groundnut oil

115 g/4 oz mushrooms, sliced

2 garlic cloves, chopped coarsely

5-cm/2-inch piece fresh galangal, sliced thinly

2 chicken breast portions (on the bone, skin on)

225 g/8 oz baby chestnut or button mushrooms, quartered

juice of ¹/2 lime

sprigs fresh flat-leaved parsley, to garnish

1 Place the dried mushrooms in a small bowl and pour over hot water to cover. Set aside to soak for 20–30 minutes. Drain the mushrooms, reserving the soaking liquid. Cut off and discard the stalks and chop the caps coarsely.

2 Pour the reserved soaking water into a saucepan with the measured water and bring to the boil. Lower the heat to a simmer.

3 Meanwhile, heat the oil in a wok and stir-fry the soaked mushrooms, sliced fresh mushrooms, garlic and galangal for 3–4 minutes. Add to the saucepan of hot water with the chicken breasts. Simmer for 10–15 minutes, until the meat comes off the bones easily.

4 Remove the chicken from the saucepan. Peel off and reserve the skin. Remove the meat from the bones, slice and reserve. Return the skin and bones to the stock and simmer for a further 30 minutes.

5 Remove the saucepan from the heat and strain the stock into a clean saucepan through a muslin-lined sieve. Bring back to the boil and add the chestnut or button mushrooms, sliced chicken and lime juice. Lower the heat and simmer for 8-10 minutes. Ladle into warmed bowls, garnish with parsley sprigs and serve immediately.

*The crisp outline of temples and palaces etches into the night sky*

# seafood and basil soup
## *tom jood ta-la sai bai hu la pa*

SERVES 4

2 tbsp vegetable or groundnut oil

4 shallots, chopped finely

2 garlic cloves, chopped

2 tsp ground turmeric

2 lemon grass stalks, snapped into three pieces

2 fresh green chillies, deseeded and sliced

3 coriander roots, chopped

3 large tomatoes, peeled (see page 24), deseeded and
   chopped, or 400 g/14 oz canned tomatoes, chopped

850 ml/1¹/₂ pints fish stock

2 tsp palm sugar or soft, light brown sugar

2 tbsp fish sauce

225 g/8 oz live mussels

12 uncooked king prawns, peeled with tails left intact

225 g/8 oz white fish fillet, skinned and cut into
   large cubes

225 g/8 oz squid, cut into rings

juice of 1 lime

3–4 sprigs fresh Thai basil

1 Heat the oil in a wok or large frying pan and
stir-fry the shallots, garlic, turmeric, lemon grass,
chillies and coriander for 1–2 minutes to release
the flavours.

2 Add the chopped tomatoes, stock, sugar and fish
sauce and simmer for 8–10 minutes.

3 Scrub the mussels under cold running water and
tug off the beards. Discard any with broken or
damaged shells and those that do not shut immediately
when sharply tapped.

4 Add the prawns, mussels, the white fish cubes and
squid to the wok or frying pan, cover and simmer
for 3–5 minutes, until the fish is cooked and the
mussels have opened. Discard any mussels that remain
closed. Stir in the lime juice and Thai basil leaves, ladle
into warmed bowls and serve immediately.

Left *Auspicious symbols are much in evidence in
Thai carving and sculpture*

Overleaf *Fiery hot chillies are to be handled with care.*

72 # rice noodles with tofu soup
## *guay tiaw tao hu*

**SERVES 4**

200 g/7 oz firm tofu, drained

vegetable or groundnut oil, for deep-frying

1 litre/1³/4 pints vegetable stock

5 spring onions, halved

1 yellow pepper, deseeded and sliced

2 celery sticks, sliced

1 small onion, sliced thinly

4 kaffir lime leaves

2 tbsp Thai soy sauce

1 tbsp Green Curry Paste (see page 31)

175 g/6 oz wide rice noodles, soaked and drained

chopped fresh coriander, to garnish

*Deep-frying tofu before using it for cooking makes it much tastier and more palatable.*

1 Using a sharp knife, cut the tofu into even cubes. Pour the oil into a wok to a depth of about 5 cm/2 inches and heat. Deep-fry the tofu, in batches, until browned all over. Remove with a slotted spoon, drain on kitchen paper and set aside.

2 Pour the stock into a saucepan and bring to the boil. Add the spring onions, yellow pepper, celery, onion, lime leaves, soy sauce and curry paste and simmer for 4–5 minutes. Add the noodles and the tofu and simmer for 2–3 minutes. Ladle into warmed bowls and serve hot topped with chopped coriander.

# duck with spring onion soup
## *ped kub ton hom*

**SERVES 4**

2 duck breasts, skin on

2 tbsp Red Curry Paste (see page 31)

2 tbsp vegetable or groundnut oil

bunch of spring onions, chopped

2 garlic cloves, crushed

5-cm/2-inch piece fresh root ginger, grated

2 carrots, sliced thinly

1 red pepper, deseeded and cut into strips

1 litre/1³/₄ pints chicken stock

2 tbsp sweet chilli sauce

3–4 tbsp Thai soy sauce

400 g/14 oz canned straw mushrooms, drained

1 Slash the skin of the duck 3 or 4 times with a sharp knife and rub in the curry paste. Cook the duck breasts, skin side down, in a wok or frying pan over a high heat for 2–3 minutes. Turn over, reduce the heat and cook for a further 3–4 minutes, until cooked through. Lift out and slice thickly. Set aside and keep warm.

2 Meanwhile, heat the oil in a wok or large frying pan and stir-fry half the spring onions, the garlic, ginger, carrots and red pepper for 2–3 minutes. Pour in the stock and add the chilli sauce, soy sauce and mushrooms. Bring to the boil, lower the heat and simmer for 4–5 minutes.

3 Ladle the soup into warmed bowls, top with the duck slices and garnish with the remaining spring onions. Serve immediately.

74

# pork with rice and egg soup
## *khao phat mu sai khai*

*This is a very thick and filling soup. Stir in the chillies and spring onions at the last moment so they just soften rather than cook. Remember that as the chillies are almost raw they will be hot.*

**SERVES 4**

350 g/12 oz pork loin, skin on

2 tsp chilli paste*

85 g/3 oz jasmine rice

850 ml/1¹/₂ pints chicken stock

1 tbsp Red Curry Paste (see page 31)

1 tsp shrimp paste

2 lemon grass stalks, snapped in half

5-cm/2-inch piece fresh root ginger, sliced thinly

2 eggs

4 spring onions, chopped

2 fresh red chillies, sliced

4 sprigs fresh Thai basil

1 Preheat the oven to 200°C/400°F/Gas Mark 6. Cut the skin away from the meat and peel back. Spread with chilli paste, then fold the skin back over the meat. Place in a roasting tin and roast for 40–45 minutes, until crisp and browned. Slice the meat thickly and then cut into thin strips. Chop the crackling. Set aside.

2 Meanwhile, rinse the rice in cold water several times until the water remains clear. Drain well.

3 Pour the stock into a saucepan, add the curry paste, shrimp paste, lemon grass and ginger and bring to the boil. Add the rice and bring back to the boil. Lower the heat and simmer for 10–12 minutes.

4 Break the eggs into the soup and once they start to set, break the yolks and stir through the rice. Simmer for a further 3–4 minutes, until the rice is cooked. Stir in the spring onions and chillies. Ladle into warmed bowls and serve topped with the hot sliced pork and pieces of crackling. Garnish with the basil sprigs.

*\*cook's tip*
You will find ready-made chilli paste in oriental food-stores and in larger supermarkets.

# spicy beef and noodle soup

## *guay tiaw tom yam nuea*

*Thailand's temples and monuments are rich in colour and eye-catching detail*

**SERVES 4**

1 litre/1³/4 pints beef stock

150 ml/¹/4 pint vegetable or groundnut oil

85 g/3 oz rice vermicelli noodles

2 shallots, sliced thinly

2 garlic cloves, crushed

2.5-cm/1-inch piece fresh root ginger, sliced thinly

225-g/8-oz piece fillet steak, cut into thin strips

2 tbsp Green Curry Paste (see page 31)

2 tbsp Thai soy sauce

1 tbsp fish sauce

chopped fresh coriander, to garnish

1 Pour the stock into a large saucepan and bring to the boil. Meanwhile, heat the oil in a wok or large frying pan. Add a third of the noodles and fry for 10–20 seconds, until they have puffed up. Lift out with tongs, drain on kitchen paper and set aside. Discard all but 2 tablespoons of the oil.

2 Add the shallots, garlic and ginger to the wok or frying pan and stir-fry for 1 minute. Add the beef and curry paste and stir-fry for a further 3–4 minutes, until tender.

3 Add the beef mixture, the uncooked noodles, soy sauce and fish sauce to the saucepan of stock and simmer for 2–3 minutes, until the noodles have swelled. Serve hot garnished with the chopped coriander and the reserved crispy noodles.

# vegetable and noodle soup
*guay tiaw nam sai puk*

**SERVES 4**

2 tbsp vegetable or groundnut oil

1 onion, sliced

2 garlic cloves, chopped finely

1 large carrot, cut into thin batons

1 courgette, cut into thin batons

115 g/4 oz broccoli, cut into florets

1 litre/1³/₄ pints vegetable stock

400 ml/14 fl oz coconut milk

3–4 tbsp Thai soy sauce

2 tbsp Red Curry Paste (see page 31)

55 g/2 oz wide rice noodles

115 g/4 oz mung or soya beansprouts

4 tbsp chopped fresh coriander

1 Heat the oil in a wok or large frying pan and stir-fry the onion and garlic for 2–3 minutes. Add the carrot, courgette and broccoli and stir-fry for 3–4 minutes, until just tender.

2 Pour in the stock and coconut milk and bring to the boil. Add the soy sauce, curry paste and noodles and simmer for 2–3 minutes, until the noodles have swelled. Stir in the beansprouts and coriander and serve immediately.

*The carving tradition can be traced back many centuries in Thailand*

# VEGETARIAN DISHES

82 It's not hard to find Thai dishes for vegetarians, since the overwhelming majority of Thai people (over 90 per cent) are Buddhists, and so don't eat meat anyway. Meat is not a major part of the Thai diet and even in dishes that do contain it only a very little is used, as it is expensive and is often bulked out with rice, noodles or vegetables.

There is an amazingly extensive array of vegetables grown in Thailand, ranging from the familiar aubergine and spring onion to the more exotic beansprouts, mung beans and bitter melon, and an assortment of greens, such as pak choi, Chinese leaves, long beans and fine beans. These ingredients are not always tasty in their own right, but once mixed together and tossed with some curry paste, they take on a whole new life and complement one another extremely well.

You can make dishes interesting by using a variety of textures as well as flavours. Most vegetarian food can be eaten with just a fork – it puts up no fight when it is eaten. That said, it is important to make sure the diner doesn't get a bowl of soggy, over-cooked and tasteless vegetables. Cooking them quickly helps to retain some crunch, keep their colour and make them interesting to eat as each one picks up a different flavour from the cooking. Marinating some ingredients, stir-frying others and adding the remaining few at the last minute, or steaming them, contribute different textures and tastes to each meal. When assembled in the serving dish, they look and taste fantastic.

### Tofu

Using tofu to provide the protein part of the meal adds a further dimension to the vegetarian meal. This versatile ingredient can be used as it is, but it tastes so much better when deep-fried first. It becomes rather like a firm omelette that is a little chewy and not at all soggy. Cut tofu into cubes and cook, in batches, in hot oil before draining on kitchen paper. It can be marinated first or can simply be added to the dish once the vegetables are cooked.

Like tofu, nuts are another useful source of protein for vegetarians, adding texture and a pleasing crunch to vegetable dishes. Try, for instance, the Sweet-and-Sour Vegetables with Cashew Nuts (see page 88), or Broccoli with Peanuts (see page 103). Nuts, too, are much tastier if they are dry-fried or grilled first, as the oil released from them increases their flavour. Watch carefully, though, as they will burn as soon as you take your eye off them.

The other plentiful ingredients in the vegetarian repertoire are rice and noodles, which of course form a significant part of the Thai diet for meat-eaters too. There are many varieties of noodles (see pages 170–71) and they all cook differently, but basically they just need soaking and are ready to eat quickly. Rice takes longer to cook, but is essential to soak up all the sauces from the curries and other dishes.

Then there are the wrappers – wonton and spring roll wrappers – that are used to enclose small parcels of food, which are steamed or fried. These require only small amounts of food as a filling and are often used as starters, but the larger spring roll wrappers can be used to make more substantial parcels of any tasty mixture. However, the filling does need to be quite dry, as too much liquid will seep out of the roll and make the oil spit and splutter during cooking.

All these different ingredients mean that it is easy to cook a fabulous vegetarian meal and not even notice the meat is missing. So you will be able to impress your vegetarian friends next time they visit. They will be thinking about eating soggy quiche again and instead you will present them with an amazing Thai feast.

*Marinating some ingredients, stir-frying others ... or steaming them, contribute different textures*

84

# vegetable parcels
## *puk hao*

*If you cannot find the small spring roll wrappers, buy the larger ones and cut them into 10-cm/ 4-inch squares.*

**SERVES 4**

2 tbsp vegetable or groundnut oil

225 g/8 oz potatoes, diced and boiled for 5 minutes

2 garlic cloves, crushed

1 onion, chopped

2 tbsp Green Curry Paste (see page 31)

55 g/2 oz frozen peas, thawed

juice of 1 lime

1/2 tsp salt

16 x 10-cm/4-inch square spring roll wrappers

1 egg, beaten

vegetable or groundnut oil, for deep-frying

sweet chilli sauce or Thai soy sauce, to serve

1 Heat the oil in a wok or frying pan and stir-fry the potatoes, garlic, onion and curry paste until lightly browned. Stir in the peas, lime juice and salt and stir-fry for 1–2 minutes. Remove from the heat.

2 Brush 1 spring roll wrapper with egg. Put a small spoonful of the potato mixture in the middle and fold up the edges to enclose the filling and make a purse-shaped parcel. Press the wrapper tightly together to seal the parcel. Repeat with the remaining wrappers and filling to make 16 small parcels.

3 Heat the oil for deep-frying in a wok. Add the vegetable parcels, in batches, and deep-fry for 3–4 minutes, until golden brown. Drain on kitchen paper and keep warm while you cook the remaining parcels. Serve hot with a bowl of chilli sauce or soy sauce for dipping.

# stuffed aubergines
## *makuea yad sai*

**SERVES 4**

8 small aubergines*

2 tbsp vegetable or groundnut oil

4 shallots, chopped finely

2 garlic cloves, crushed

2 fresh red chillies, deseeded and chopped

1 courgette, chopped coarsely

115 g/4 oz creamed coconut, chopped

few Thai basil leaves, chopped

small handful of fresh coriander, chopped

4 tbsp Thai soy sauce


*to serve*

rice with chopped spring onions

sweet chilli sauce

1 Preheat the oven to 200°C/400°F/Gas Mark 6. Put the aubergines on a roasting tin and cook for 8–10 minutes, until just softened. Cut in half and scoop out the flesh, reserving the shells.

2 Heat the oil in a wok or large frying pan and fry the shallots, garlic and chilli for 2–3 minutes before adding the courgettes and aubergine flesh. Add the creamed coconut, the herbs and soy sauce and simmer for 3–4 minutes.

3 Share the mixture between the aubergine shells. Return to the oven for 5–10 minutes until hot and serve immediately with rice and sweet chilli sauce.

*cook's tip*
If you can only find large aubergines, one half per person would probably be enough.

88 # sweet-and-sour vegetables with cashew nuts
*preow wan puk sai tua ob*

**SERVES 4**

1 tbsp vegetable or groundnut oil

1 tsp chilli oil

2 onions, sliced

2 carrots, sliced thinly

2 courgettes, sliced thinly

115 g/4 oz broccoli, cut into florets

115 g/4 oz button mushrooms, sliced

115 g/4 oz small pak choi, halved

2 tbsp palm sugar or soft, light brown sugar

2 tbsp Thai soy sauce

1 tbsp rice vinegar

55 g/2 oz cashew nuts

1 Heat both the oils in a wok or frying pan and stir-fry the onions for 1–2 minutes, until they start to soften.

2 Add the carrots, courgettes and broccoli and stir-fry for 2–3 minutes. Add the mushrooms, pak choi, sugar, soy sauce and rice vinegar and stir-fry for 1–2 minutes.

3 Meanwhile, dry-fry or toast the cashews. Sprinkle the cashews over the stir-fry and serve immediately.

# mixed mushroom stir-fry
## *pud hed ruem*

**SERVES 4**

2 tbsp vegetable or groundnut oil

6 spring onions, sliced

1 tbsp Green Curry Paste (see page 31)

115 g/4 oz shiitake mushrooms, halved

115 g/4 oz oyster mushrooms

115 g/4 oz button mushrooms

115 g/4 oz field mushrooms, sliced

2 tbsp Thai soy sauce

1 tsp palm sugar or soft, light brown sugar

225 g/8 oz canned water chestnuts, drained, rinsed
   and sliced

55 g/2 oz beansprouts

cooked noodles, to serve

1 Heat the oil in a wok or frying pan and stir-fry the spring onions for 30 seconds. Add the curry paste and stir-fry for 1–2 minutes. Add all the mushrooms and stir-fry over a high heat until they are tender.

2 Add the soy sauce, sugar, water chestnuts and beansprouts and cook for 1–2 minutes, until heated through and just tender. Serve hot with noodles.

90
# aubergine and bean curry
*kaeng ped ma khure sai tua*

Look for the pea aubergines that are very popular in
Thai cooking, but if you cannot find them, use just
the more familiar purple ones.

### SERVES 4

2 tbsp vegetable or groundnut oil

1 onion, chopped

2 garlic cloves, crushed

2 fresh red chillies, deseeded and chopped

1 tbsp Red Curry Paste (see page 31)

1 large aubergine, cut into chunks

115 g/4 oz pea or small aubergines

115 g/4 oz baby broad beans

115 g/4 oz fine French beans

300 ml/$^1$/$_2$ pint vegetable stock

55 g/2 oz creamed coconut, chopped

3 tbsp Thai soy sauce

1 tsp palm sugar or soft, light brown sugar

3 kaffir lime leaves, torn coarsely

4 tbsp chopped fresh coriander

1 Heat the oil in a wok or large frying pan and fry the
onion, garlic and chillies for 1-2 minutes. Stir
in the curry paste and cook for 1-2 minutes.

2 Add the aubergines and cook for 3–4 minutes, until
starting to soften. (You may need to add a little
more oil as aubergines soak it up quickly.) Add all the
beans and stir-fry for 2 minutes.

3 Pour in the stock and add the creamed coconut, soy
sauce, sugar and lime leaves. Bring gently to the
boil and cook until the coconut has dissolved. Stir in
the coriander and serve hot.

# carrot and pumpkin curry
## *kaeng ped carrot kub phuk*

*When pumpkins are not available, use butternut squash instead. Peel, remove the seeds and cut into cubes before cooking.*

**SERVES 4**

150 ml/¼ pint vegetable stock

2.5-cm/1-inch piece fresh galangal, sliced

2 garlic cloves, chopped

1 lemon grass stalk (white part only), chopped finely

2 fresh red chillies, deseeded and chopped

4 carrots, peeled and cut into chunks

225 g/8 oz pumpkin, peeled, deseeded and cut
    into cubes

2 tbsp vegetable or groundnut oil

2 shallots, chopped finely

3 tbsp Yellow Curry Paste

400 ml/14 fl oz coconut milk

4–6 sprigs fresh Thai basil

25 g/1 oz toasted pumpkin seeds, to garnish

*for the Yellow Curry Paste*

3 small fresh orange or yellow chillies, chopped coarsely

3 large garlic cloves, chopped coarsely

4 shallots, chopped coarsely

3 tsp ground turmeric

1 tsp salt

12–15 black peppercorns

1 lemon grass stalk (white part only), chopped coarsely

2.5-cm/1-inch piece fresh root ginger, chopped

1 Pour the stock into a large saucepan and bring to the boil. Add the galangal, half the garlic, the lemon grass and chillies and simmer for 5 minutes. Add the carrots and pumpkin and simmer for 5–6 minutes, until tender.

2 To make the curry paste*, put all the ingredients into a food processor or blender and process to a thick paste, scraping down the sides occasionally and making sure they are well combined.

3 Meanwhile, heat the oil in a wok or frying pan and stir-fry the shallots and the remaining garlic for 2–3 minutes. Add the curry paste and stir-fry for 1–2 minutes.

4 Stir the shallot mixture into the saucepan and add the coconut milk and basil. Simmer for 2–3 minutes. Serve hot, sprinkled with the toasted pumpkin seeds.

*\*cook's tip*
The Yellow Curry Paste can be stored in the refrigerator and used when required. It will keep for up to 3 weeks. Alternatively, you could fill the spaces in an ice cube tray and freeze – use a cube at a time after thawing for about 30 minutes beforehand.

Overleaf *Statues representing Buddha are built on a breathtaking scale.*

96

# onion, potato and red pepper curry
*kaeng ped mun fa rung sai hom yai, phrik yhuak*

1 Heat the oil in a wok or large frying pan and stir-fry the onions, garlic, ginger and chilli for 2–3 minutes. Add the curry paste and stir-fry over a low heat for 2–3 minutes.

2 Add the potatoes, peppers, stock and salt and cook for 3–4 minutes, until all the vegetables are tender. Stir in the coriander and serve immediately.

**SERVES 4**

2 tbsp vegetable or groundnut oil

2 red onions, sliced

2 garlic cloves, chopped finely

5-cm/2-inch piece fresh root ginger, chopped finely

1 red chilli, deseeded and chopped

1 tbsp Red Curry Paste (see page 31)

225 g/8 oz potatoes, cut into cubes, boiled for 5 minutes and drained

2 red peppers, deseeded and diced

300 ml/$^1$/$_2$ pint vegetable stock

1 tsp salt

4 tbsp chopped fresh coriander

# mixed greens curry 97
## *kaeng khiao wan ruam*

**SERVES 4**

2 tbsp vegetable or groundnut oil

1 fresh green chilli, deseeded and chopped

6 spring onions, sliced

3 tbsp Green Curry Paste (see page 31)

115 g/4 oz pak choi

115 g/4 oz Chinese leaves

115 g/4 oz spinach

115 g/4 oz asparagus

3 celery sticks, sliced diagonally

3 tbsp Thai soy sauce

1 tsp palm sugar or soft, light brown sugar

juice of 1 lime

boiled jasmine rice, to serve

1 Heat the oil in a wok or large frying pan and stir-fry the chilli and spring onions for 1–2 minutes. Add the curry paste and stir-fry for 2–3 minutes.

2 Add the pak choi, Chinese leaves, spinach, asparagus and celery and stir-fry for 3–4 minutes, until just tender.

3 Add the soy sauce, sugar and lime juice and cook for 30 seconds to heat through. Serve immediately with boiled jasmine rice.

98
# tofu and green vegetable curry
*kaeng khiao wan tao hu*

**SERVES 4**

vegetable or groundnut oil, for deep-frying

225 g/8 oz firm tofu, drained and cut into cubes

2 tbsp vegetable or groundnut oil

1 tbsp chilli oil

2 fresh green chillies, deseeded and sliced

2 garlic cloves, crushed

6 spring onions, sliced

2 medium courgettes, cut into batons

1/2 cucumber, peeled, deseeded and sliced

1 green pepper, deseeded and sliced

1 small head broccoli, cut into florets

55 g/2 oz fine French beans, halved

55 g/2 oz frozen peas, thawed

300 ml/1/2 pint vegetable stock

55 g/2 oz creamed coconut, chopped

2 tbsp Thai soy sauce

1 tsp palm sugar or soft, light brown sugar

4 tbsp chopped fresh parsley, to garnish

1 Heat the oil for deep-frying in a frying pan and carefully lower in the tofu cubes, in batches, and cook for 2–3 minutes, until golden brown. Remove with a slotted spoon and drain on kitchen paper.

2 Heat the other oils in a wok and stir-fry the chillies, garlic and spring onions for 2–3 minutes. Add the courgettes, cucumber, green pepper, broccoli and French beans and stir-fry for a further 2–3 minutes.

3 Add the peas, stock, coconut, soy sauce and sugar. Cover and simmer for 2–3 minutes, until all the vegetables are tender and the coconut has dissolved.

4 Stir in the tofu and serve immediately, sprinkled with the parsley.

# courgette and cashew nut curry
## *kaeng courgette med mamuang*

**SERVES 4**

2 tbsp vegetable or groundnut oil

6 spring onions, chopped

2 garlic cloves, chopped

2 fresh green chillies, deseeded and chopped

450 g/1 lb courgettes, cut into thick slices*

115 g/4 oz shiitake mushrooms, halved

50 g/2 oz beansprouts

75 g/3 oz cashew nuts, toasted or dry-fried

few Chinese chives, chopped

4 tbsp Thai soy sauce

1 tsp fish sauce

rice or noodles, to serve

1 Heat the oil in a wok or large frying pan and fry the onions, garlic and chillies for 1–2 minutes, until softened but not browned.

2 Add the courgettes and mushrooms and cook for 2–3 minutes until tender.

3 Add the beansprouts, nuts, chives and both sauces and stir-fry for 1–2 minutes.

4 Serve hot with rice or noodles.

*cook's tip*
Try to find small courgettes. Slices of larger ones might need to be cut in half before cooking.

# broccoli with peanuts

*pud thai broccoli sai tua ob*

**SERVES 4**

3 tbsp vegetable or groundnut oil

1 lemon grass stalk, chopped coarsely

2 fresh red chillies, deseeded and chopped

2.5-cm/1-inch piece fresh root ginger, grated

3 kaffir lime leaves, torn coarsely

3 tbsp Green Curry Paste (see page 31)

1 onion, chopped

1 red pepper, deseeded and chopped

350 g/12 oz broccoli, cut into florets

115 g/4 oz fine French beans

55 g/2 oz unsalted peanuts

1 Put 2 tablespoons of the oil, the lemon grass, chillies, ginger, lime leaves and curry paste into a food processor or blender and process to a paste.

2 Heat the remaining oil in a wok, add the spice paste, onion and pepper and stir-fry for 2–3 minutes, until the vegetables start to soften.

3 Add the broccoli and French beans, cover and cook over a low heat, stirring occasionally, for 4–5 minutes, until tender.

4 Meanwhile, toast or dry-fry the peanuts until lightly browned. Add them to the broccoli mixture and toss together. Serve immediately.

*Vivid colour is everywhere in the streets – and on the waterways – of Thailand*

## 104 vegetables with tofu and spinach
### *pud puk sai tao hu*

1 Heat the oil in a frying pan and deep-fry the tofu cubes, in batches, for 4–5 minutes, until crisp and browned. Remove with a slotted spoon and drain on kitchen paper.

2 Heat 2 tablespoons of the oil in a wok or frying pan and stir-fry the onions, garlic and chilli for 1–2 minutes, until they start to soften. Add the celery, mushrooms, corn cobs and red pepper and stir-fry for 3–4 minutes, until they soften.

3 Stir in the curry paste and coconut milk and gradually bring to the boil. Add the sugar and soy sauce and then the spinach. Cook, stirring constantly, until the spinach has wilted. Serve immediately, topped with the tofu.

**SERVES 4**

vegetable or groundnut oil, for deep-frying

225 g/8 oz firm tofu, drained and cut into cubes

2 tbsp vegetable or groundnut oil

2 onions, chopped

2 garlic cloves, chopped

1 fresh red chilli, deseeded and sliced

3 celery sticks, sliced diagonally

225 g/8 oz mushrooms, sliced thickly

115 g/4 oz baby corn cobs, cut in half

1 red pepper, deseeded and cut into strips

3 tbsp Red Curry Paste (see page 31)

400 ml/14 fl oz coconut milk

1 tsp palm sugar or soft, light brown sugar

2 tbsp Thai soy sauce

225 g/8 oz baby spinach leaves

*Shrine at the Grand Palace in Bangkok. Visitors are expected to dress and behave with respect when visiting shrines and temples*

MAIN MEALS

Just as starters are not part of Thai culinary culture, the Thai people don't have main courses either, simply because they usually serve all their dishes together and eat them at the same time, making meals very sociable occasions. When I selected the recipes in this chapter I had in mind the way many people in the West organize their meals.

A lot of us eat breakfast, a light snack at lunchtime and have the main meal in the evening – precisely when everyone comes home exhausted.

Part of the attraction of Thai food is the speed with which it is cooked and the fact that some of the preparation can be done in advance. Ideal for weary workers who still want to eat a delicious meal! Meat can be cut up and left in a marinade, onions and garlic can be peeled and bagged, vegetables trimmed, cut to size and left in a bag or box. Rice and noodles can be weighed, ready to prepare on your return. Once you are home, the meal can be cooked in next

Meals in Thailand will usually include an assortment of salads as well, but these have their own chapter (see page 196–231). I think we tend to like a hot meal when we come home in the evening and in this chapter we concentrate on hot dishes. However, a lot of the dishes you'll find in this section can be cooked and served cold or eaten cold the following day.

Most of these recipes would be served with rice or noodles to soak up sauces and to add a modifying flavour to the spicier dishes so that there is a mixture of hot and cooler tastes. (Of course we all have differing appetites and spice tolerance-levels so adjust the amounts to suit your family or guests.)

*The seasonings used in Thai food mean that by its very nature it will be hot, spicy and tasty. There are lots of curries – not blow-your-brains out ... but delicate, tongue-tingling ones*

to no time, so you will spend as little time in the kitchen as possible. For those who like to cook, there is great pleasure and relaxation to be had from preparing food, so there is something for everyone in this style of cooking – quick and easy meals for some; fish to skin and cube, prawns to peel and curry pastes to make for others.

The seasonings used in Thai food mean that by its very nature it will be hot, spicy and tasty. There are lots of curries – not blow-your-brains-out Indian vindaloos, but delicate, tongue-tingling ones that affect every area of your mouth. As well as these types of recipe, I have included other traditional and recognizable dishes – but with a Thai twist.

Chilli sauce or soy sauce can be served separately with meals so people can use them as condiments or as dips if they like.

What do you drink with Thai food? I would suggest jasmine tea, Singha beer, fruit juice or a fruity white wine. Remember: if you find the food hot, wait until you've finished before you sip a cold drink. Drinking as you eat only makes the spices seem hotter.

It is great fun learning a new skill and style of cooking, as well as finding out about another country and its ways of eating. You will soon become accustomed to the vibrant flavours and be cooking Thai dishes more often. The only trouble will be that your friends will also enjoy your cooking so much, they will be round for dinner every night!

110

# green chicken curry
*kaeng khiao wan gai*

**SERVES 4**

1 tbsp vegetable or groundnut oil

1 onion, sliced

1 garlic clove, chopped finely

2–3 tbsp Green Curry Paste (see page 31)

400 ml/14 fl oz coconut milk

150 ml/¼ pint chicken stock

4 kaffir lime leaves

4 skinned, boned chicken breasts, cut into cubes

1 tbsp fish sauce

2 tbsp Thai soy sauce

grated rind and juice of ½ lime

1 tsp palm sugar or soft, light brown sugar

4 tbsp chopped fresh coriander, to garnish

1 Heat the oil in a wok or large frying pan and stir-fry the onion and garlic for 1–2 minutes, until starting to soften. Add the curry paste and stir-fry for 1–2 minutes.

2 Add the coconut milk, stock and lime leaves, bring to the boil and add the chicken. Lower the heat and simmer gently for 15–20 minutes, until the chicken is tender.

3 Add the fish sauce, soy sauce, lime rind and juice and sugar. Cook for 2–3 minutes, until the sugar has dissolved. Serve immediately, garnished with chopped coriander.

*Thailand's tropical climate is ideal for the coconut palm, and the nuts and milk are plentifully used in Thai cuisine*

# fish in coconut 113
## *kaeng ka-ti pla*

*Visual reminders abound of the many battles Thailand has known throughout its history*

SERVES 4

2 tbsp vegetable or groundnut oil

6 spring onions, chopped coarsely

2.5-cm/1-inch piece fresh root ginger, grated

2–3 tbsp Red Curry Paste (see page 31)

400 ml/14 fl oz coconut milk

150 ml/$^1$/$_4$ pint fish stock

4 kaffir lime leaves

1 lemon grass stalk, broken in half

350 g/12 oz white fish fillets, skinned and cut
    into chunks

225 g/8 oz squid rings and tentacles

225 g/8 oz large cooked peeled prawns

1 tbsp fish sauce

2 tbsp Thai soy sauce

4 tbsp chopped fresh Chinese chives

boiled jasmine rice with chopped fresh coriander,
    to serve

1 Heat the oil in a wok or large frying pan and stir-fry the spring onions and ginger for 1–2 minutes. Add the curry paste and stir-fry for 1–2 minutes.

2 Add the coconut milk, fish stock, lime leaves and lemon grass. Bring to the boil, then lower the heat and simmer for 1 minute.

3 Add the fish, squid and prawns and simmer for 2–3 minutes, until the fish is cooked. Add the fish and soy sauces and stir in the chives. Serve immediately with jasmine rice with fresh coriander stirred through it.

114
# chicken and peanut curry
*kaeng ped gai sai tao ob*

**SERVES 4**

*for the Penang Curry Paste*

8 large dried red chillies

2 tsp shrimp paste

3 shallots, chopped

5-cm/2-inch piece fresh galangal, chopped

8 garlic cloves, chopped

4 tbsp chopped coriander root

3 lemon grass stalks (white part only), chopped

grated rind of 1 lime

1 tbsp fish sauce

2 tbsp vegetable or groundnut oil

1 tsp salt

6 tbsp crunchy peanut butter

1 tbsp vegetable or groundnut oil

2 red onions, sliced

2 tbsp Penang Curry Paste

400 ml/14 fl oz coconut milk

150 ml/$^1$/4 pint chicken stock

4 kaffir lime leaves, torn coarsely

1 lemon grass stalk, chopped finely

6 skinned, boned chicken thighs, chopped

1 tbsp fish sauce

2 tbsp Thai soy sauce

1 tsp palm sugar or soft, light brown sugar

50 g/1$^3$/4 oz unsalted peanuts, roasted and chopped,
  plus extra to garnish

175 g/6 oz fresh pineapple, chopped coarsely

15-cm/6-inch piece cucumber, peeled, deseeded and
  sliced thickly, plus extra to garnish

1 First make the curry paste. Cut off and discard the chilli stalks and place the chillies in a bowl. Cover with hot water and set aside to soak for 30–45 minutes. Wrap the shrimp paste in foil and grill or dry-fry for 2–3 minutes, turning once or twice. Put the chillies and their soaking water into a blender or food processor. Add the shrimp paste, shallots, galangal, garlic, coriander root and lemon grass and process until finely chopped. Add the lime rind, fish sauce, oil and salt and process again. Add the peanut butter and process to make a thick paste, scraping down the sides occasionally.*

2 Heat the oil in a wok and stir-fry the onions for 1 minute. Add the curry paste and stir-fry for 1–2 minutes.

3 Pour in the coconut milk and stock. Add the lime leaves and lemon grass and simmer for 1 minute. Add the chicken and gradually bring to the boil. Simmer for 8–10 minutes, until the chicken is tender.

4 Stir in the fish sauce, soy sauce and sugar and simmer for 1–2 minutes. Stir in the peanuts, pineapple and cucumber and cook for 30 seconds. Serve immediately, sprinkled with extra nuts and cucumber.

*cook's tip

The Penang Curry Paste can be refrigerated or frozen in the same way as the Yellow Curry Paste (see page 93).

# stuffed omelette parcels 117
## *kai yud sai*

**SERVES 4**

8 large eggs

4 tbsp water

2 large fresh red chillies, deseeded and chopped

1/2 tsp salt

1 tbsp vegetable or groundnut oil

4 spring onions, chopped

2 tbsp Red Curry Paste (see page 31)

2 skinned, boned chicken breasts, cubed

115 g/4 oz shiitake mushrooms, chopped

*to garnish*

chopped fresh coriander

chopped fresh Chinese chives

1 Beat the eggs with the water, the chillies and salt. Pour a quarter of the mixture into a 20 cm/8 inch frying pan and cook over a low heat until set. Slide the omelette out on to a plate and make 3 more in the same way.

2 Meanwhile, heat the oil in a wok and stir-fry the spring onions with the curry paste for 1–2 minutes. Add the chicken and mushrooms and stir-fry for 3–4 minutes, until cooked through.

3 Divide the chicken mixture equally between the omelettes, piling it up in the centre. Fold all the sides over the filling to enclose it and make a square parcel. Place the omelettes, seam side down, in a single layer in a steamer. Cover with a lid and cook over boiling water for 4–5 minutes until hot. Transfer to warmed plates, sprinkle the chopped herbs over the top and serve immediately.

118

# barbecue chicken
## *gai yang*

**SERVES 4**

1 litre/1³/₄ pints chicken stock

8 chicken thighs

1 tbsp lime juice

2 garlic cloves, crushed

2 tbsp Thai soy sauce

1 tbsp fish sauce

2 tbsp chilli sauce

1 Bring the stock to the boil in a large wok. Add the chicken and simmer for 8–10 minutes, until cooked. Remove with a slotted spoon and set aside to cool.

2 Put the cold chicken in a shallow dish. Combine the lime juice, garlic, soy sauce, fish sauce and chilli sauce in a bowl and spoon the mixture over the chicken, turning to coat. Cover with clingfilm and chill for 2–3 hours.

3 Cook the chicken thighs over hot coals*, turning them frequently and brushing with the marinade, for 8–10 minutes, until browned and crisp. Serve hot or cold.

*cook's tip

You can also cook the chicken under the grill or on a ridged griddle pan. It is important that the meat is cooked all the way through – this is why it is cooked before barbecuing.

# pork with peppers

*pud moo phrik-thai*

**SERVES 4**

1 tbsp vegetable or groundnut oil

1 tbsp chilli oil

450 g/1 lb pork fillet, sliced thinly

2 tbsp green chilli sauce

6 spring onions, sliced

2.5-cm/1-inch piece fresh root ginger, sliced thinly

1 red pepper, deseeded and sliced

1 yellow pepper, deseeded and sliced

1 orange pepper, deseeded and sliced

1 tbsp fish sauce

2 tbsp Thai soy sauce

juice of $1/2$ lime

4 tbsp chopped fresh parsley

cooked flat rice noodles, to serve

1 Heat both the oils in a wok. Add the pork, in batches, and stir-fry until browned all over. Remove with a slotted spoon and reserve.

2 Add the chilli sauce, spring onions and ginger to the wok and stir-fry for 1–2 minutes. Add the peppers and stir-fry for 2–3 minutes.

3 Return the meat to the wok, stir well and add the fish sauce, soy sauce and lime juice. Cook for a further 1–2 minutes, then stir in the parsley and serve with flat rice noodles.

120 # red curry pork with peppers
## *kaeng moo*

**SERVES 4**

2 tbsp vegetable or groundnut oil

1 onion, roughly chopped

2 garlic cloves, chopped

450 g/1 lb pork fillet, sliced thickly

1 red pepper, deseeded and cut into squares

175 g/6 oz mushrooms, quartered

2 tbsp Red Curry Paste (see page 31)

115 g/4 oz creamed coconut, chopped

300 ml/1/2 pint pork or vegetable stock

2 tbsp Thai soy sauce

4 tomatoes, peeled (see page 24), deseeded and chopped

handful of fresh coriander, chopped

boiled noodles or rice, to serve

1 Heat the oil in a wok or large frying pan and fry the onion and garlic for 1–2 minutes, until they are softened but not browned.

2 Add the pork slices and stir-fry for 2–3 minutes until browned all over. Add the pepper, mushrooms and curry paste.

3 Dissolve the coconut in the hot stock and add to the wok with the soy sauce. Bring to the boil and simmer for 4–5 minutes until the liquid has reduced and thickened.

4 Add the tomatoes and coriander and cook for 1–2 minutes before serving with noodles or rice.

*The haunting sound of monastery bells rung by the Buddhist monks is one of the evocative memories of a visit to Thailand*

# spicy beef with potato
## *pud ped nuea sai mun fa rung*

SERVES 4

450 g/1 lb beef fillet

2 tbsp Thai soy sauce

2 tbsp fish sauce

2 tbsp vegetable or groundnut oil

3–4 coriander roots, chopped

1 tbsp crushed black peppercorns

2 garlic cloves, chopped

1 tbsp palm sugar or soft, light brown sugar

350 g/12 oz potatoes, diced

150 ml/¼ pint water

**bunch of spring onions, chopped**

**225 g/8 oz baby spinach leaves**

**cooked rice or noodles, to serve**

1 Cut the beef into thick slices and place in a shallow dish. Put the soy sauce, fish sauce, 1 tablespoon of the oil, the coriander roots, peppercorns, garlic and sugar in a food processor and process to a thick paste. Scrape the paste into the dish and toss the beef to coat. Cover with clingfilm and set aside to marinate in the fridge for at least 3 hours, preferably overnight.

2 Heat the remaining oil in a wok. Lift the beef out of the marinade, reserving the marinade, and fry for 3-4 minutes on each side, until browned. Add the reserved marinade and the potatoes with the measured water and gradually bring to the boil. Simmer for 6-8 minutes, or until the potatoes are tender.

3 Add the spring onions and spinach. Cook gently until the greens have wilted. Serve immediately with rice or noodles.

*Intricately adorned dragons are a typical theme in Thai art*

124

# coconut beef curry
## *kaeng ped ka-ti nuea*

**SERVES 4**

*for the Mussaman Curry Paste*

4 large dried red chillies

2 tsp shrimp paste

3 shallots, chopped finely

3 garlic cloves, chopped finely

2.5-cm/1-inch piece fresh galangal, chopped finely

2 lemon grass stalks (white part only), chopped finely

2 cloves

1 tbsp coriander seeds

1 tbsp cumin seeds

seeds from 3 cardamom pods

1 tsp black peppercorns

1 tsp salt

1 tbsp ground coriander

1 tbsp ground cumin

3 tbsp Mussaman Curry Paste

150 ml/$^1$/$_4$ pint water

75 g/2$^3$/$_4$ oz creamed coconut

450 g/1 lb beef fillet, cut into strips

400 ml/14 fl oz coconut milk

50 g/1$^3$/$_4$ oz unsalted peanuts, chopped finely

2 tbsp fish sauce

1 tsp palm sugar or soft, light brown sugar

4 kaffir lime leaves

boiled rice with chopped fresh coriander, to serve

1 First make the curry paste*. Cut off and discard the chilli stalks and place the chillies in a bowl. Cover with hot water and set aside to soak for 30–45 minutes. Wrap the shrimp paste in foil and grill or dry-fry for 2–3 minutes, turning once or twice. Remove from the grill or frying pan. Dry-fry the shallots, garlic, galangal, lemon grass, cloves, coriander, cumin and cardamom seeds over a low heat, stirring frequently, for 3–4 minutes, until lightly browned. Transfer to a food processor and process until finely ground. Add the chillies and their soaking water, peppercorns and salt, and process again. Add the shrimp paste and process again to a smooth paste, scraping down the sides as necessary.

2 Combine the coriander, cumin and curry paste in a bowl. Pour the measured water into a saucepan, add the creamed coconut and heat until it has dissolved. Add the curry paste mixture and simmer for 1 minute.

3 Add the beef and simmer for 6–8 minutes, then add the coconut milk, peanuts, fish sauce and sugar. Simmer gently for 15–20 minutes, until the meat is tender.

4 Add the lime leaves and simmer for 1–2 minutes. Serve the curry hot with rice with freshly chopped coriander stirred through it.

*\*cook's tip*
The Mussaman Curry Paste can be refrigerated or frozen in the same way as the Yellow Curry Paste (see page 93).

# monkfish with lime and chilli sauce
## *yum pla*

**SERVES 4**

4 x 115 g/4 oz monkfish fillets

25 g/1 oz rice flour or cornflour

6 tbsp vegetable or groundnut oil

4 garlic cloves, crushed

2 large fresh red chillies, deseeded and sliced

2 tsp palm sugar or soft, light brown sugar

juice of 2 limes

grated rind of 1 lime

boiled rice, to serve

1 Toss the fish in the flour, shaking off any excess. Heat the oil in a wok and fry the fish on all sides until browned and cooked through, taking care when turning not to break it up.

2 Lift the fish out of the wok and keep warm. Add the garlic and chillies and stir-fry for 1–2 minutes, until they have softened.

3 Add the sugar, the lime juice and rind and 2–3 tablespoons of water and bring to the boil. Simmer gently for 1–2 minutes, then spoon the mixture over the fish. Serve immediately with rice.

Left *In contrast to the simple life led by Buddhist monks, temples and shrines are frequently embellished in gold*

Overleaf *Temple ruins are a common sight in the north of Thailand which in the past was the most easily conquered part of the country*

# gingered chicken kebabs
## *kebab gai khing*

**SERVES 4**

3 skinned, boned chicken breasts, cut into cubes

juice of 1 lime

2.5-cm/1-inch piece root ginger, peeled and chopped

1 fresh red chilli, deseeded and sliced

2 tbsp vegetable or groundnut oil

1 onion, sliced

2 garlic cloves, chopped

1 aubergine, cut into chunks

2 courgettes, cut into thick slices

1 red pepper, deseeded and cut into squares

2 tbsp Red Curry Paste (see page 31)

2 tbsp Thai soy sauce

1 tsp palm sugar or soft, light brown sugar

boiled rice with chopped coriander, to serve

1 Put the chicken cubes in a shallow dish. Mix the lime, ginger and chilli together and pour over the chicken pieces. Stir gently to coat. Cover and chill for at least 3 hours to marinate.

2 Thread the chicken pieces onto soaked wooden skewers and cook under a hot grill for 3–4 minutes, turning often, until cooked through.

3 Meanwhile, heat the oil in a wok or large frying pan and fry the onion and garlic for 1–2 minutes until softened but not browned. Add the aubergine, courgette and pepper and cook for 3–4 minutes until cooked but still firm. Add the curry paste, soy sauce and sugar and cook for 1 minute.

4 Serve hot with boiled rice, stirred through with chopped coriander.

*Thailand's interior includes some spectacular sights that are little known outside the country*

## 132 minced chicken skewers
*gai ping*

**SERVES 4**

450 g/1 lb minced chicken

1 onion, chopped finely

1 fresh red chilli, deseeded and chopped

2 tbsp Red Curry Paste (see page 31)

1 tsp palm sugar or soft, light brown sugar

1 tsp ground coriander

1 tsp ground cumin

1 egg white

8 lemon grass stalks

boiled rice with chopped spring onion, to serve

1 Combine the chicken, onion, chilli, curry paste and sugar in a bowl and stir well to make a thick paste. Stir in the ground coriander, cumin and egg white and mix again.

2 Divide the mixture into 8 equal portions and squeeze them around each of the lemon grass stalks. Arrange on a grill pan and cook under a high heat, turning frequently, until browned and cooked through. Serve hot with the rice with the spring onion stirred through it.

*Red and gold are frequently used colours in Thai ornamentation*

# pork and crab meatballs
## *mu, pu pan kon thot*

**SERVES 6**

225 g/8 oz pork fillet, chopped finely

170 g/5¾ oz canned crab meat, drained

3 spring onions, chopped finely

1 garlic clove, chopped finely

1 tsp Red Curry Paste (see page 31)

1 tbsp cornflour

1 egg white

vegetable or groundnut oil, for deep-frying

boiled rice, to serve

*for the sauce*

1 tbsp vegetable or groundnut oil

2 shallots, chopped

1 garlic clove, crushed

2 large fresh red chillies, deseeded and chopped

4 spring onions, chopped

3 tomatoes, chopped coarsely

1 Put the pork and crab meat into a bowl and mix together. Add the spring onions, garlic, curry paste, cornflour and egg white and beat well to make a thick paste. With damp hands shape the mixture into walnut-sized balls.

2 Heat the oil in a wok and deep-fry the balls, in batches, for 3–4 minutes, turning frequently, until golden brown and cooked. Drain on kitchen paper and keep warm.

3 To make the sauce, heat the oil in a wok and stir-fry the shallots and garlic for 1–2 minutes. Add the chillies and spring onions and stir-fry for 1–2 minutes, then add the tomatoes. Stir together quickly, then spoon the sauce over the pork and crab balls. Serve immediately with rice.

*Parts of rural Thailand are stunning, but most tourists head for the main cities and beaches*

# 136 crispy pork dumplings
## *moo krob*

**SERVES 4**

350 g/12 oz minced pork

2 tbsp finely chopped fresh coriander

1 garlic clove, crushed

1 fresh green chilli, deseeded and chopped

3 tbsp cornflour

1 egg white

1/2 tsp salt

16 wonton wrappers

1 tbsp water

vegetable or groundnut oil, for frying

chilli sauce, to serve

1 Put the pork in a bowl and beat in the coriander, garlic, chilli, 1 tablespoon of the cornflour, the egg white and salt. Beat together to a thick, smooth texture. With damp hands shape into 16 equal portions and roll into balls.

2 Put a pork ball in the centre of each wonton wrapper. Make a paste by mixing the remaining cornflour with 1 tablespoon of water. Brush the edges of the wrappers with the cornflour paste and gather them up around the filling to make half into small, sack-like parcels, and the rest into triangular shapes.

3 Arrange the dumplings in a single layer (in batches if need be) in the top of a steamer and cook over boiling water for 10–15 minutes, until the meat is cooked through.

4 Heat the oil in a wok or large frying pan and carefully drop the parcels into it. Deep-fry for 2–3 minutes, until golden brown and crisp. Drain on kitchen paper and serve hot with chilli sauce.

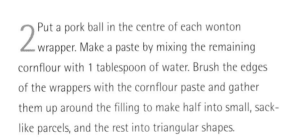

*The fabulous gold shrines and temples make a visit to Thailand an unforgettable experience*

# mussaman curry
## *kaeng mussaman*

**SERVES 4**

1 tbsp vegetable or groundnut oil

450 g/1 lb beef topside, cut into cubes

2 tbsp Mussaman Curry Paste (see page 124)

2 large onions, cut into wedges

2 large potatoes, cut into chunks

400 ml/14 fl oz coconut milk

150 ml/1/4 pint water

2 cardamom pods

2 tbsp tamarind paste

2 tsp palm sugar or soft, light brown sugar

75 g/2³/₄ oz unsalted peanuts, toasted or dry-fried

1 fresh red chilli, sliced thinly

boiled rice, to serve

1 Heat the oil in a wok and fry the meat, in batches, until browned all over. Remove with a slotted spoon and set aside.

2 Add the curry paste to the wok and stir-fry for 1–2 minutes. Add the onions and potatoes and stir-fry for 4–5 minutes, until golden brown. Remove with a slotted spoon and set aside.

3 Pour the coconut milk into the wok with the measured water and bring to the boil. Lower the heat and simmer for 8–10 minutes.

4 Return the meat and cooked vegetables to the wok. Add the cardamoms, tamarind paste and sugar and simmer for 15–20 minutes, until the meat is tender. Stir in the peanuts and chilli and serve with rice.

*Northern Thailand is where the early Thai kingdoms first developed, and shrines and temples abound*

140 # prawns with noodles
## *guay tiaw kung*

**SERVES 4**

450 g/1 lb uncooked tiger prawns

1 tbsp vegetable or groundnut oil

3 shallots, chopped finely

2 garlic cloves, chopped finely

2.5-cm/1-inch piece fresh root ginger, sliced thinly

400 ml/14 fl oz canned coconut milk

1 tbsp Green Curry Paste (see page 31)

3–4 fresh Thai basil leaves

1 tsp palm sugar or soft, light brown sugar

225 g/8 oz flat rice noodles

2 tsp sesame oil

2 tbsp sesame seeds, toasted

sprigs fresh Thai basil, to garnish

1 Remove and discard the heads and peel the prawns. Cut a slit along the back of each and remove and discard the dark vein.

2 Heat the oil in a wok and stir-fry the shallots, garlic and ginger for 2–3 minutes. Add the coconut milk and curry paste and simmer for 2–3 minutes.

3 Add the prawns, basil leaves and sugar and cook until the prawns turn pink.

4 Meanwhile, cook the noodles in boiling water according to the packet instructions, then drain well. Stir in the sesame oil and seeds, garnish with the sprigs of basil and serve immediately with the prawns.

*Attention to colour and detail is evident everywhere in Thailand*

# fish curry with rice noodles
## *guay tiaw kaeng pla*

**SERVES 4**

2 tbsp vegetable or groundnut oil

1 large onion, chopped

2 garlic cloves, chopped

75 g/3 oz button mushrooms

225 g/8 oz monkfish, cut into cubes,
    each about 2.5 cm/1 inch

225 g/8 oz salmon fillets, cut into cubes,
    each about 2.5 cm/1 inch

225 g/8 oz cod, cut into cubes,
    each about 2.5 cm/1 inch

2 tbsp Red Curry Paste (see page 31)

400 g/14 oz canned coconut milk

handful of fresh coriander, chopped

1 tsp palm sugar or soft, light brown sugar

1 tsp fish sauce

115 g/4 oz rice noodles

3 spring onions, chopped

50 g/2 oz beansprouts

few Thai basil leaves

1 Heat the oil in a wok or large frying pan and gently fry the onion, garlic and mushrooms until softened but not browned.

2 Add the fish, curry paste and coconut milk and bring gently to the boil. Simmer for 2–3 minutes before adding half the the coriander, the sugar and fish sauce. Keep warm.

3 Meanwhile, soak the noodles for 3–4 minutes (check the packet instructions) or until tender and drain well through a colander. Put the colander and noodles over a saucepan of simmering water. Add the spring onions, beansprouts and most of the basil and steam on top of the noodles for 1–2 minutes or until just wilted.

4 Pile the noodles onto warmed serving plates and top with the fish curry. Scatter the remaining coriander and basil over the top and serve immediately.

# mixed seafood curry
## *pok tak*

SERVES 4

1 tbsp vegetable or groundnut oil

3 shallots, chopped finely

2.5-cm/1-inch piece fresh galangal, peeled and
    sliced thinly

2 garlic cloves, chopped finely

400 ml/14 fl oz canned coconut milk

2 lemon grass stalks, snapped in half

4 tbsp fish sauce

2 tbsp chilli sauce

225 g/8 oz uncooked tiger prawns, peeled

225 g/8 oz baby squid, cleaned and sliced thickly

225 g/8 oz salmon fillet, skinned and cut into chunks

175 g/6 oz tuna steak, cut into chunks

225 g/8 oz fresh mussels, scrubbed and debearded

fresh Chinese chives, to garnish

boiled rice, to serve

1 Heat the oil in a large wok and stir-fry the shallots, galangal and garlic for 1–2 minutes, until they start to soften. Add the coconut milk, lemon grass, fish sauce and chilli sauce. Bring to the boil, lower the heat and simmer for 1–2 minutes.

2 Add the prawns, squid, salmon and tuna and simmer for 3–4 minutes, until the prawns have turned pink and the fish is cooked.

3 Add the mussels and cover with a lid. Simmer for 1–2 minutes, until they have opened. Discard any mussels that remain closed. Garnish with Chinese chives and serve immediately with rice.

*At a temple, hardly any
surface is left unadorned*

# STIR-FRIED MEALS

148 The wok is the essential cooking pot used in Far Eastern cookery. It is hugely versatile, comes in several sizes, and is cheap to buy. They do need a bit of looking after, but doesn't that apply to any favourite tool in the kitchen? It is much harder to stir-fry in an ordinary frying pan, as there is no room to toss the food or push vegetables to one side while you add other ingredients.

Looking at our photographs, you may think the woks look huge, but they need to be big for precisely these reasons – room to toss and stir-fry the food, keeping it moving as it cooks.

Gas is the best fuel for stir-frying, as the flames can lick around the outside of the wok, heating the sides as well as the base, but most flat-based woks will work on an electric hob. You will need to buy a specialist wok if you cook on a ceramic or an induction hob.

The secret of successful stir-frying is that there is no secret – it's all totally obvious. The wok and oil need to be hot, but not smoking, the meat and vegetables should all be cut to a similar size so they cook in the same time, and the hardest, toughest food should be cooked first, adding the softer, more delicate things at the last moment. The wet sauces and pastes are usually added once the vegetables and meat are almost cooked. So it's easy and fast, ideal for starving students and people in a hurry. Fast, furious and fun, even the kids can manage it – under supervision.

However, it is essential that you have everything prepared before you begin cooking. Choose fresh, crisp young vegetables. Bendy old carrots will not become crunchy during cooking and soggy spring onions will always be just that. Peel and chop or slice all the vegetables. It doesn't matter whether you cut them into thin batons or just slice them, but make

sure that they are all a similar size and that you trim off any tatty ends. It's a good idea to assemble the ingredients in the order in which I list them, because that is the order in which they are cooked.

Meat is usually sliced thinly and then cut into strips. Cut across the grain of beef to break up the tough fibres and to help make it tender. The most popular meat is chicken and this does cook quickly, and it is less fibrous than lamb or beef. It is more economical to buy boned breast portions and to pull off the skin yourself rather than use prepared breasts. Keep an eye open for corn-fed chicken as it has more flavour. As with other meats, it will need to be sliced or cut into cubes.

Have all the sauces and pastes ready to hand so

# *The secret of successful stir-frying is that there is no secret – it's all totally obvious*

there won't be any rushing around at the last minute. Don't hesitate to use ready-made curry pastes to speed things along, but be prepared for the strong smell and slightly stinging eyes when stirring in these prepared spicy additions to the ingredients (the same applies to fresh chillies).

I have given precise measurements for sauces and pastes but if you cook by eye, that's fine. However, remember to taste as you go and keep adjusting the flavours, adding more soy sauce or chilli sauce, for example. (You won't need much salt as the soy sauce and spice pastes are quite salty anyway.)

Have any fresh basil or coriander chopped to add to the wok just before serving so they have time to add flavour, but not disintegrate. So you are all set, now it's just go, go, go ... dinner in 10 minutes!

150 # shredded chicken and mixed mushrooms
*gai sai hed ruam*

**SERVES 4**

2 tbsp vegetable or groundnut oil

2 skinned, boned chicken breasts

1 red onion, sliced

2 garlic cloves, chopped finely

2.5-cm/1-inch piece fresh root ginger, grated

115 g/4 oz baby button mushrooms

115 g/4 oz shiitake mushrooms, halved

115 g/4 oz chestnut mushrooms, sliced

2–3 tbsp Green Curry Paste (see page 31)

2 tbsp Thai soy sauce

4 tbsp chopped fresh parsley

boiled noodles or rice, to serve

1 Heat the oil in a wok and fry the chicken on all sides until lightly browned and cooked through. Remove with a slotted spoon, shred into even-sized pieces and set aside.

2 Pour off any excess oil, then stir-fry the onion, garlic and ginger for 1–2 minutes, until softened. Add the mushrooms and stir-fry for 2–3 minutes, until they start to brown.

3 Add the curry paste, soy sauce and shredded chicken to the wok and stir-fry for 1–2 minutes. Stir in the parsley and serve immediately with noodles or rice.

*Samtors, Thailand's 3-wheeler taxis, known as* tuk-tuks, *are one way to get around*

# prawns with spring onions and straw mushrooms

## *kung sai tun-hom la hed*

**SERVES 4**

2 tbsp vegetable or groundnut oil

bunch of spring onions, chopped

2 garlic cloves, chopped finely

175 g/6 oz creamed coconut, chopped coarsely

2 tbsp Red Curry Paste (see page 31)

450 ml/$^3/_4$ pint fish stock

2 tbsp fish sauce

2 tbsp Thai soy sauce

6 sprigs fresh Thai basil

400 g/14 oz canned straw mushrooms, drained

350 g/12 oz large cooked peeled prawns

boiled jasmine rice, to serve

1 Heat the oil in a wok and stir-fry the spring onions and garlic for 2–3 minutes. Add the creamed coconut, red curry paste and stock and heat gently until the coconut has dissolved.

2 Stir in the fish sauce and soy sauce, then add the basil, mushrooms and prawns. Gradually bring to the boil and serve immediately with jasmine rice.

*The carved stone faces of gods and emperors record Thailand's history*

## 154 cauliflower and beans with cashew nuts
### *daung-ka-lum sai tau khiao, tao ob*

**SERVES 4**

1 tbsp vegetable or groundnut oil

1 tbsp chilli oil

1 onion, chopped

2 garlic cloves, chopped

2 tbsp Red Curry Paste (see page 31)

1 small cauliflower, cut into florets

175 g/6 oz long beans, cut into 7.5-cm/3-inch lengths

150 ml/¼ pint vegetable stock

2 tbsp Thai soy sauce

50 g/1¾ oz toasted cashew nuts, to garnish

1 Heat both the oils in a wok and stir-fry the onion and garlic until softened. Add the curry paste and stir-fry for 1–2 minutes.

2 Add the cauliflower and beans and stir-fry for 3–4 minutes, until softened. Pour in the stock and soy sauce and simmer for 1–2 minutes. Serve immediately, garnished with the cashews.

# duck with mixed peppers 155
*ped kub phrik thai*

**SERVES 4**

1 tbsp vegetable or groundnut oil

2 duck breasts, skin on

1 onion, sliced

2 garlic cloves, chopped

1 red pepper, deseeded and chopped

1 green pepper, deseeded and chopped

1 yellow pepper, deseeded and chopped

4 tomatoes, peeled (see page 24), deseeded
  and chopped

150 ml/¼ pint stock

3 tbsp Thai soy sauce

boiled noodles, to serve

1 Heat the oil in a wok and fry the duck breasts over a high heat until crisp and brown. Turn over and fry until cooked through. Lift out and keep warm.

2 Pour off any excess fat and stir-fry the onion and garlic for 2–3 minutes, until softened and lightly browned.

3 Add the peppers and stir-fry for 2–3 minutes, until tender. Add the tomatoes, stock and soy sauce and simmer for 1–2 minutes. Transfer to a serving plate. Slice the duck thickly and arrange on top, spooning any sauce over it. Serve immediately with noodles.

# ginger chicken with noodles

*guay tiaw gai sai khing*

**SERVES 4**

2 tbsp vegetable or groundnut oil

1 onion, sliced

2 garlic cloves, chopped finely

5-cm/2-inch piece fresh root ginger, sliced thinly

2 carrots, sliced thinly

4 skinned, boned chicken breasts, cut
  into cubes

300 ml/1/2 pint chicken stock

4 tbsp Thai soy sauce

225 g/8 oz canned bamboo shoots, drained and rinsed

75 g/23/4 oz flat rice noodles

*for the garnish*

4 spring onions, chopped

4 tbsp chopped fresh coriander

1 Heat the oil in a wok and stir-fry the onion, garlic, ginger and carrots for 1–2 minutes, until softened. Add the chicken and stir-fry for 3–4 minutes, until the chicken is cooked through and lightly browned.

2 Add the stock, soy sauce and bamboo shoots and gradually bring to the boil. Simmer for 2–3 minutes. Meanwhile, soak the noodles in boiling water for 6–8 minutes. Drain well. Garnish with the spring onions and coriander and serve immediately, with the chicken stir-fry.

Right *Gifts and flowers are offered up to sacred shrines*

Overleaf *Homes on the rivers of Thailand's central plains are built on stilts*

160 # mixed vegetables with quick-fried basil
*pud puk ruam ka-preow tord grob*

**SERVES 4**

2 tbsp vegetable or groundnut oil

2 garlic cloves, chopped

1 onion, sliced

115 g/4 oz baby corn cobs, cut in half diagonally

$1/2$ cucumber, peeled, halved, deseeded and sliced

225 g/8 oz canned water chestnuts, drained and rinsed

55 g/2 oz mangetout, trimmed

115 g/4 oz shiitake mushrooms

1 red pepper, deseeded and sliced thinly

1 tbsp palm sugar or soft, light brown sugar

2 tbsp Thai soy sauce

1 tbsp fish sauce

1 tbsp rice vinegar

boiled rice, to serve

*for the quick-fried basil*

**vegetable or groundnut oil, for frying**

**8-12 sprigs fresh Thai basil**

1 Heat the oil in a wok and stir-fry the garlic and onion for 1-2 minutes. Add the corn cobs, cucumber, water chestnuts, mangetout, mushrooms and red pepper and stir-fry for 2–3 minutes, until starting to soften.

2 Add the sugar, soy sauce, fish sauce and vinegar and gradually bring to the boil. Simmer for 1–2 minutes.

3 Meanwhile, heat the oil for the basil in a wok or frying pan and, when hot, add the basil sprigs. Fry for 20–30 seconds, until crisp. Remove with a slotted spoon and drain on kitchen paper.

4 Garnish the vegetable stir-fry with the crispy basil and serve immediately, with the boiled rice.

162 # chicken with yellow curry sauce
## *gai pud phung ka-ri*

**SERVES 4**

*for the spice paste*

6 tbsp Yellow Curry Paste (see page 93)

150 ml/¼ pint natural yogurt

400 ml/14 fl oz water

handful of fresh coriander, chopped

handful of fresh Thai basil leaves, shredded

*for the stir-fry*

2 tbsp vegetable or groundnut oil

2 onions, cut into thin wedges

2 garlic cloves, chopped finely

2 skinned, boned chicken breasts, cut
   into strips

175 g/6 oz baby corn cobs, halved lengthways

*to garnish*

chopped fresh coriander

shredded fresh basil

1 To make the spice paste, stir-fry the yellow curry paste in a wok for 2–3 minutes, then stir in the yogurt, water and herbs. Bring to the boil, then simmer for 2–3 minutes.

2 Meanwhile, heat the oil in a wok and stir-fry the onions and garlic for 2–3 minutes. Add the chicken and corn cobs and stir-fry for 3–4 minutes, until the meat and corn are tender.

3 Stir in the spice paste and bring to the boil. Simmer for 2–3 minutes, until heated through. Serve immediately, garnished with extra herbs if liked.

# pork with mixed green beans
## *pud tua sai mu*

1 Heat the oil in a wok and stir-fry the shallots, pork, galangal and garlic until lightly browned.

2 Add the stock, chilli sauce and peanut butter and stir until the peanut butter has melted. Add all the beans and simmer for 3–4 minutes. Serve hot with crispy noodles.

**SERVES 4**

2 tbsp vegetable or groundnut oil

2 shallots, chopped

225 g/8 oz pork fillet, sliced thinly

2.5-cm/1-inch piece fresh galangal, sliced thinly

2 garlic cloves, chopped

300 ml/1/2 pint chicken stock

4 tbsp chilli sauce

4 tbsp crunchy peanut butter

115 g/4 oz fine French beans

115 g/4 oz frozen broad beans

115 g/4 oz runner beans, sliced

crispy noodles, to serve

164

# beef with onions and broccoli
*pud nuea sai hom-yai la thai broccoli*

**SERVES 4**

2 tbsp vegetable or groundnut oil

2 tbsp Green Curry Paste (see page 31)

2 x 175 g/6 oz sirloin steaks, sliced thinly

2 onions, sliced

6 spring onions, chopped

2 shallots, chopped finely

225 g/8 oz broccoli, cut into florets

400 ml/14 fl oz coconut milk

3 kaffir lime leaves, chopped coarsely

4 tbsp chopped fresh coriander

few Thai basil leaves

1 Heat the oil in a wok and stir-fry the curry paste for 1–2 minutes. Add the meat, in batches if necessary, and stir-fry until starting to brown.

2 Add the onions, spring onions and shallots and stir-fry for 2–3 minutes. Add the broccoli and stir-fry for 2–3 minutes.

3 Pour in the coconut milk, add the lime leaves and bring to the boil. Simmer gently for 8–10 minutes, until the meat is tender. Stir in the coriander and basil and serve immediately.

*The Asian elephant, a native of Thailand, is an auspicious symbol*

# squid and red peppers

*pud pla-muk sai phrik-deang*

**SERVES 4**

*for the spice paste*

2 tbsp vegetable or groundnut oil

1 tbsp chilli oil with shrimp

2 shallots, chopped

2–3 large fresh red chillies, deseeded and
    chopped coarsely

2 tbsp ground coriander

2 tbsp ground cumin

2.5-cm/1-inch piece fresh root ginger, chopped

1 tbsp finely chopped lemon grass

3–4 coriander roots, chopped

1 tsp salt

1 tsp palm sugar or soft, light brown sugar

*for the stir-fry*

2 red peppers, deseeded and diced

150 ml/¼ pint natural yogurt

750 g/1 lb 10 oz squid, cleaned and sliced

juice of 1 lime

115 g/4 oz creamed coconut, chopped

150 ml/¼ pint hot water

1 Put all the ingredients for the spice paste into a food processor and process until chopped finely.

2 Scrape the spice paste into a wok and stir-fry gently for 3–4 minutes. Add the red peppers and stir-fry for 1–2 minutes.

3 Add the yogurt and bring to the boil. Add the squid and simmer for 2–3 minutes, then stir in the lime juice, coconut and water. Simmer for a further 1–2 minutes, until the coconut dissolves. Serve immediately.

*Entire meals are cooked in the bottom of the flat boats that ply the waterways*

NOODLES & RICE

170 Noodles are probably one of the quickest foods to prepare in the modern world. The larger supermarkets are now full of numerous dried varieties, often ready-flavoured, that only need to be covered in boiling water and left for a couple of minutes to swell. Absolutely fabulous for young children and students, noodles are cheap, easy to cook and taste delicious.

In Thailand it's somewhat different. Noodles are by no means only a quick snack: they're a culinary institution. There are a great many varieties and hundreds of recipes use them as the main ingredient. The type of noodle depends on the flour used to make them – it could be rice flour, mung bean flour or wheat flour (even though the country does not count wheat among its staple crops) – whereas the name of the noodle depends on the thickness of the strips.

One of the most popular varieties of noodle is the flat, dried rice-flour noodles (*kuay tiaw*), which are widely available, even in supermarkets. Then there are the spaghetti-like fresh rice flour noodles (*kanom jeen*), which are rather like the type used in Malaysia and Singapore. Check out the chiller cabinets in your local supermarket for fresh egg noodles that are quick to cook and are great for adding to soups. Dried wheat-flour noodles are thinner, flatter and creamier in colour than the white dried rice vermicelli (*sen mee*), which are also sometimes known as rice-stick noodles. Dried transparent or jelly noodles (*woon sen*) are used predominantly in soups and salads, rice sticks (*sen lek*) are the thinnest ones available, and the best-known noodles are the thin and wiry rice vermicelli (*kuay tiaw jeen*). These are fun to drop into hot oil and watch puff up. They are rather like prawn crackers in texture but do not have a lot of taste.

dash of chilli oil or with soy sauce poured over them. Or they can be topped with peanuts, as in the popular dish Pad Thai (see page 172), or a few stir-fried vegetables. Because noodles are so quick to prepare and season, street hawkers have traditionally sold them in a variety of ways: soaking them in meat stock, topping them with pieces of stir-fried meat or prawns, or sprinkling them with sugar or hot chilli flakes. Pad Thai is traditionally prepared as a dish of stir-fried noodles, cooked quickly in very hot oil in a hot wok, and mixed together with prawns, beef, eggs, tofu, vegetables and a variety of seasonings including garlic and spring onions. However, it can also make the most stunning vegetarian dish using only the tofu and vegetables.

## Noodles taste wonderful as a snack or a meal on their own, with a dash of chilli oil or with soy sauce poured over them

Noodles vary in thickness as well. The popular egg noodle (*kuay tiaw–be mee*) is approximately 2 mm/$^1$/16 inch thick, vermicelli are much thinner and the flatter types are obviously wider. All dried noodles can be found in specialist Thai and Chinese foodstores, and the larger supermarkets stock an increasing range. The majority can also be found fresh if you seek out the more specialist shops.

Noodles should be soaked or cooked in boiling water, but not for very long. If they are overcooked they will fall apart and become bland and soggy. Some types just need covering with boiling water and leaving for a couple of minutes before draining and using, but do check the packet instructions or ask for advice in the foodstore.

Rather than putting ingredients in with the noodles, as you can when cooking rice, it is more effective to wait until the noodles have been drained before you decide how to flavour them. Noodles taste wonderful as a snack or meal on their own, with a

Along with noodles, rice is the other basic staple food eaten in Thailand, as it is in most countries throughout the Far East – and indeed the Middle East. It is easy and cheap to grow and is produced in vast amounts. Thailand has long been famous for its jasmine rice, which is a popular high-grade variety and, as most of it is exported, it is easily available in the West. This type is often called fragrant or scented rice because of the fabulous smell it produces while it is cooking. Glutinous rice, which is much stickier, can also be used in many sweet recipes. The 'stickiness' results from the amount of starch in the rice grains, so if you do want sticky rice, don't rinse off all the starch before cooking: soak it overnight, then steam for 10–15 minutes.

# pad thai
## *phat thai*

*The best known of all Thai noodle dishes.*

**SERVES 4**

225 g/8 oz thick rice-stick noodles

2 tbsp vegetable or groundnut oil

2 garlic cloves, chopped

2 fresh red chillies, deseeded and chopped

175 g/6 oz pork fillet, sliced thinly

115 g/4 oz uncooked prawns, peeled and chopped

8 fresh Chinese chives, chopped

2 tbsp fish sauce

juice of 1 lime

2 tsp palm sugar or soft, light brown sugar

2 eggs, beaten

115 g/4 oz beansprouts

4 tbsp chopped fresh coriander

115 g/4 oz unsalted peanuts, chopped, plus extra to serve

crispy fried onions, to serve

1 Soak the noodles in warm water for 10 minutes, drain well and set aside.

2 Heat the oil in a wok and stir-fry the garlic, chillies and pork for 2–3 minutes. Add the prawns and stir-fry for a further 2–3 minutes.

3 Add the chives and noodles, then cover and cook for 1–2 minutes. Add the fish sauce, lime juice, sugar and eggs. Cook, stirring and tossing constantly to mix in the eggs.

4 Stir in the beansprouts, coriander and peanuts and serve with small dishes of crispy fried onions and extra chopped peanuts.

174 # pork with vegetables
*pud puk sai moo*

**SERVES 4**

8 tbsp vegetable or groundnut oil

115 g/4 oz rice vermicelli noodles

4 belly pork rashers, sliced thickly

1 red onion, sliced

2 garlic cloves, chopped

2.5-cm/1-inch piece fresh root ginger, sliced thinly

1 large fresh red chilli, deseeded and chopped

115 g/4 oz baby corn cobs, halved lengthways

1 red pepper, deseeded and sliced

175 g/6 oz broccoli, cut into florets

150 g/5$^{1}/_{2}$ oz jar black bean sauce

115 g/4 oz beansprouts

1 Heat the oil in a wok and fry the rice noodles, in batches, for 15-20 seconds, until they puff up. Remove with a slotted spoon, drain on kitchen paper and set aside.

2 Pour off all but 2 tablespoons of the oil and stir-fry the pork, onion, garlic, ginger and chilli for 4–5 minutes, or until the meat has browned.

3 Add the corn cobs, red pepper and broccoli and stir-fry for 3–4 minutes, until the vegetables are just tender. Stir in the black bean sauce and beansprouts, cook for a further 2–3 minutes. Serve immediately, topped with the crispy noodles.

# stir-fried rice with green vegetables
## *khao phat puk*

**SERVES 4**

225 g/8 oz jasmine rice

2 tbsp vegetable or groundnut oil

1 tbsp Green Curry Paste (see page 31)

6 spring onions, sliced

2 garlic cloves, crushed

1 courgette, cut into thin batons

115 g/4 oz long beans

175 g/6 oz asparagus, trimmed

1 tbsp fish sauce

3–4 fresh Thai basil leaves

1 Cook the rice in lightly salted boiling water for 12–15 minutes, drain well, then cool thoroughly and chill overnight.

2 Heat the oil in a wok and stir-fry the curry paste for 1 minute. Add the spring onions and garlic and stir-fry for 1 minute.

3 Add the courgette, beans and asparagus and stir-fry for 3–4 minutes, until just tender. Break up the rice and add it to the wok. Cook, stirring constantly for 2–3 minutes, until the rice is hot. Stir in the fish sauce and basil leaves. Serve hot.

176 # egg-fried rice with vegetables and crispy onions
*khao-khai pak horm-tord*

**SERVES 4**

4 tbsp vegetable or groundnut oil

2 garlic cloves, chopped finely

2 fresh red chillies, deseeded and chopped

115 g/4 oz mushrooms, sliced

50 g/2 oz mangetout, halved

50 g/2 oz baby sweetcorn, halved

3 tbsp Thai soy sauce

1 tbsp palm sugar or soft, light brown sugar

few Thai basil leaves

350 g/12 oz rice, cooked and cooled*

2 eggs, beaten

2 onions, sliced

1 Heat half the oil in a wok or large frying pan and fry the garlic and chillies for 2–3 minutes.

2 Add the mushrooms, mangetout and sweetcorn and stir-fry for 2–3 minutes before adding the soy sauce, sugar and basil. Stir in the rice.

3 Push the mixture to one side of the wok and add the eggs to the base and stir until lightly set before combining into the rice mixture.

4 Heat the remaining oil in another frying pan and fry the onions until crispy and brown. Serve the rice topped with the onions.

*cook's tip

The rice must be cold when it is added to the wok, otherwise the egg will combine with it to make a congealed mass.

# curried noodles with shrimps and straw mushrooms
## *guay tiaw kung sai hed*

179

**SERVES 4**

1 tbsp vegetable or groundnut oil

3 shallots, chopped

1 fresh red chilli, deseeded and chopped

1 tbsp Red Curry Paste (see page 31)

1 lemon grass stalk (white part only), chopped finely

225 g/8 oz cooked peeled prawns

400 g/14 oz canned straw mushrooms, drained

2 tbsp fish sauce

2 tbsp Thai soy sauce

225 g/8 oz fresh egg noodles

fresh coriander, chopped, to garnish

1 Heat the oil in a wok and stir-fry the shallots and chilli for 2–3 minutes. Add the curry paste and lemon grass and stir-fry for 2–3 minutes.

2 Add the prawns, mushrooms, fish sauce and soy sauce and stir well to mix.

3 Meanwhile, cook the noodles in boiling water for 3–4 minutes, drain and transfer to warmed plates. Top with the prawn curry, sprinkle the coriander over and serve immediately.

*The distinctive saffron-coloured robes may be seen on statues as well as worn by Buddhist monks*

# 180 spicy noodles with mushroom spring rolls
## *guay tiaw tom yam kub po pia hed*

**SERVES 4**

2 tbsp vegetable or groundnut oil

1 small onion, chopped finely

225 g/8 oz mushrooms, chopped

1 tbsp Red Curry Paste (see page 31)

1 tbsp Thai soy sauce

1 tbsp fish sauce

8 square spring roll wrappers

vegetable or groundnut oil, for deep-frying

225 g/8 oz quick-cook noodles

1 garlic clove, chopped

6 spring onions, chopped

1 red pepper, deseeded and chopped

1 tbsp ground coriander

1 tbsp ground cumin

1 Heat 1 tablespoon of the oil in a wok and stir-fry the onion and mushrooms until crisp and browned. Add the curry paste, soy sauce and fish sauce and stir-fry for 2–3 minutes. Remove the wok from the heat.

2 Spoon an eighth of the mixture across one of the spring roll wrappers and roll up, folding the sides over the filling to enclose it.

3 Heat the oil for deep-frying in a wok or frying pan and deep-fry the spring rolls, 4 at a time, until crisp and browned. Drain on kitchen paper and keep warm.

4 Meanwhile, put the noodles in a bowl, cover with boiling water and leave to swell.

5 Heat the remaining oil in the wok and stir-fry the garlic, spring onions and red pepper for 2–3 minutes. Stir in the coriander and cumin, then drain the noodles and add them to the wok. Toss together and serve topped with the spring rolls.

# chicken with vegetables and coriander rice

## *khao man gai*

**SERVES 4**

2 tbsp vegetable or groundnut oil

1 red onion, chopped

2 garlic cloves, chopped

2.5-cm/1-inch piece root ginger, peeled and chopped

2 skinned, boned chicken breasts, cut into strips

115 g/4 oz button mushrooms

400 g/14 oz canned coconut milk

50 g/2 oz sugar snap peas, trimmed and halved
  lengthways

2 tbsp soy sauce

1 tbsp fish sauce

*for the rice*

1 tbsp vegetable or groundnut oil

1 red onion, sliced

350 g/12 oz rice, cooked and cooled

250 g/8 oz pak choy, torn into large pieces

handful of fresh coriander, chopped

2 tbsp Thai soy sauce

1 Heat the oil in a wok or large frying pan and fry the onion, garlic and ginger together for 1–2 minutes.

2 Add the chicken and mushrooms and fry over a high heat until browned. Add the coconut milk, sugar snap peas and sauces and bring to the boil. Simmer gently for 4–5 minutes until tender.

3 Heat the oil for the rice in a separate wok or large frying pan and fry the onion until softened but not browned. Add the cooked rice, pak choy and fresh coriander and heat gently until the leaves have wilted and the rice is hot. Sprinkle over the soy sauce and serve immediately with the chicken.

Overleaf *Vivid green kaffir limes, and their leaves, provide a key flavouring in Thai cuisine*

# prawns with coconut rice
## *khao ka-ti khung*

### SERVES 4

115 g/4 oz dried Chinese mushrooms

2 tbsp vegetable or groundnut oil

6 spring onions, chopped

55 g/2 oz desiccated coconut

1 fresh green chilli, deseeded and chopped

225 g/8 oz jasmine rice

150 ml/¼ pint fish stock

400 ml/14 fl oz coconut milk

350 g/12 oz cooked peeled prawns

6 sprigs fresh Thai basil

1 Place the mushrooms in a small bowl, cover with hot water and set aside to soak for 30 minutes. Drain, then cut off and discard the stalks and slice the caps.

2 Heat 1 tablespoon of the oil in a wok and stir-fry the spring onions, coconut and chilli for 2–3 minutes, until lightly browned. Add the mushrooms and stir-fry for 3–4 minutes.

3 Add the rice and stir-fry for 2–3 minutes, then add the stock and bring to the boil. Lower the heat and add the coconut milk. Simmer for 10–15 minutes, until the rice is tender. Stir in the prawns and basil, heat through and serve.

# rice with seafood and squid
## *khao sai khung la pha-muk*

**SERVES 4**

2 tbsp vegetable or groundnut oil

3 shallots, chopped finely

2 garlic cloves, chopped finely

225 g/8 oz jasmine rice

300 ml/½ pint fish stock

4 spring onions, chopped

2 tbsp Red Curry Paste (see page 31)

225 g/8 oz baby squid, cleaned and sliced thickly

225 g/8 oz white fish fillets, skinned and cut into cubes

225 g/8 oz salmon fillets, skinned and cut into cubes

4 tbsp chopped fresh coriander

1 Heat 1 tablespoon of the oil in a wok and stir-fry the shallots and garlic for 2–3 minutes, until softened. Add the rice and stir-fry for 2–3 minutes.

2 Add a ladleful of the stock and simmer, adding more stock as needed, for 12–15 minutes, until tender. Transfer to a dish, cool and chill overnight.

3 Heat the remaining oil in a wok and stir-fry the spring onions and curry paste for 2–3 minutes. Add the squid and fish and stir-fry gently to avoid breaking up the fish. Stir in the rice and coriander, heat through gently and serve.

# fish curry
## *kaeng ped pla*

SERVES 4

juice of 1 lime

4 tbsp fish sauce

2 tbsp Thai soy sauce

1 fresh red chilli, deseeded and chopped

350 g/12 oz monkfish fillet, cut into cubes

350 g/12 oz salmon fillets, skinned and cut into cubes

400 ml/14 fl oz coconut milk

3 kaffir lime leaves

1 tbsp Red Curry Paste (see page 31)

1 lemon grass stalk (white part only), chopped finely

225 g/8 oz jasmine rice, boiled

4 tbsp chopped fresh coriander

1 Combine the lime juice, half the fish sauce and the soy sauce in a shallow, non-metallic dish. Add the chilli and the fish, stir to coat, cover with clingfilm and chill for 1–2 hours, or overnight.

2 Bring the coconut milk to the boil in a saucepan and add the lime leaves, curry paste, the remaining fish sauce and the lemon grass. Simmer gently for 10–15 minutes.

3 Add the fish and the marinade and simmer gently for 4–5 minutes, until the fish is cooked. Serve hot with boiled rice with chopped coriander stirred through it.

*The warm waters of the Andaman Sea are a rich source of seafood*

# stir-fried rice noodles with marinated fish
## *guay tiaw pla*

**SERVES 4**

450 g/1 lb monkfish or cod, cubed

225 g/8 oz salmon fillets, cubed

2 tbsp vegetable or groundnut oil

2 fresh green chillies, deseeded and chopped

grated rind and juice of 1 lime

1 tbsp fish sauce

115 g/4 oz wide rice noodles

2 tbsp vegetable or groundnut oil

2 shallots, sliced

2 garlic cloves, chopped finely

1 fresh red chilli, deseeded and chopped

2 tbsp Thai soy sauce

2 tbsp chilli sauce

1 Place the fish in a shallow bowl. To make the marinade, mix the oil, green chillies, lime juice and rind and fish sauce together and pour over the fish. Cover and chill for 2 hours.

2 Put the noodles in a bowl and cover with boiling water. Leave for 8–10 minutes (check the packet instructions) and drain well.

3 Heat the oil in a wok or large frying pan and fry the shallots, garlic and red chilli until lightly browned. Add the soy sauce and chilli sauce. Add the fish and the marinade to the wok and stir-fry gently for 2–3 minutes until cooked through.

4 Add the drained noodles and stir gently. Sprinkle with coriander and serve immediately.

192

# beef with fresh noodles
## *guay tiaw nuea*

### SERVES 4

6 dried black cloud Chinese mushrooms

2 tbsp vegetable or groundnut oil

2 x 225 g/8 oz sirloin steaks, sliced thickly

1 onion, cut into thin wedges

2 garlic cloves, chopped

1 green pepper, deseeded and chopped

3 celery sticks, sliced

2 tbsp Green Curry Paste (see page 31)

300 ml/$\frac{1}{2}$ pint beef stock

4 tbsp black bean sauce

225 g/8 oz fresh egg noodles

4 tbsp chopped fresh parsley

1 Put the mushrooms in a bowl, cover with boiling water and set aside to soak for 30 minutes. Drain. Break up any larger pieces.

2 Heat the oil in a wok and stir-fry the steak over a high heat until browned. Add the mushrooms, onion, garlic, pepper and celery and stir-fry for 3–4 minutes. Add the curry paste, beef stock and black bean sauce and stir-fry for 2–3 minutes.

3 Meanwhile, cook the noodles in boiling water for 3–4 minutes, drain well and stir into the wok. Sprinkle the parsley over and stir. Serve immediately.

*The temple of the Emerald Buddha in Bangkok*

# egg-fried rice with chicken

## *khao phat gai sai khai*

**SERVES 4**

225 g/8 oz jasmine rice

3 skinned, boned chicken breasts, cut into cubes

400 ml/14 fl oz canned coconut milk

50 g/1³⁄4 oz creamed coconut, chopped

2–3 coriander roots, chopped

thinly pared rind of 1 lemon

1 fresh green chilli, deseeded and chopped

3 fresh Thai basil leaves

1 tbsp fish sauce

1 tbsp oil

3 eggs, beaten

*for the garnish*

fresh chives

sprigs fresh coriander

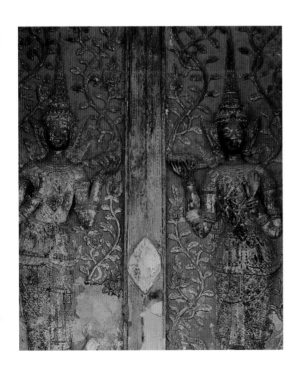

1 Cook the rice in boiling water for 12–15 minutes, drain well, then cool and chill overnight.

2 Put the chicken into a saucepan and cover with the coconut milk. Add the creamed coconut, coriander roots, lemon rind and chilli and bring to the boil. Simmer for 8–10 minutes, until the chicken is tender. Remove from the heat. Stir in the basil and fish sauce.

3 Meanwhile, heat the oil in a wok and stir-fry the rice for 2–3 minutes. Pour in the eggs and stir until they have cooked and mixed with the rice. Line 4 small pudding basins or ramekins with clingfilm and pack with the rice. Turn out carefully onto serving plates and remove the clingfilm. Garnish with long chives and sprigs of coriander. Serve with the chicken.

*Sculptures and murals adorn every Thai temple*

# SALADS

198 Often called 'yam' dishes, salads accompany most Thai meals and usually consist of a mixture of either raw vegetables or ones that have been cooked quickly, which are served with some crunch still in them. Salads are sometimes served as an appetizer when they are offered just before a meal as something to snack on before the main courses arrive.

That said, as most dishes are usually served almost at the same time at the Thai table, rather than as separate courses, any salads immediately become part of the meal.

Typically, a Thai salad should include hot and intense flavours. These act to stimulate the taste buds ready for the dishes that follow. Chillies, soy and fish sauces as well as coriander, garlic and palm sugar all play an important part in many of the salads included here. The combination of these ingredients enhances the meat, fish or vegetables that are being prepared and cooked, adding that extra dimension of flavour that is quintessentially Thai.

We eat a lot of salads in the West but our traditional dishes are vastly different from the type of salads served in the East. Ours tend to be blander and more leafy, and include only a few ingredients that are tossed in a dressing, whereas Thai salads, like many other Thai dishes, are meant to be spicy and mouth-tingling. This departure from the traditions of our cuisine is in part what makes Thai food such fun to cook and eat. Exposure to different styles of food from around the world has made us much more adventurous in our tastes and cooking skills these days and it's good to experience and experiment with the culinary styles of another culture. Even people who don't relish cooking but like to eat Thai food in restaurants are willing to try new and unusual tastes. But as more foodstores stock the exotic and unfamiliar ingredients these days, we can all have a go at tackling Thai food, including salads, at home.

As always, it is vital to use fresh, crispy vegetables because they provide the best flavour and texture, whether they are cooked or eaten raw. Limp or soggy vegetables will produce a soggy salad, so choose the best you can find. Cut everything to a similar size for stir-frying to ensure that they cook evenly and, even if you are serving a cold salad, think about cutting all ingredients into manageable, bite-sized pieces so they are easier and a pleasure to eat. Use your biggest wok or frying pan to stir-fry the vegetables so there is plenty of room for tossing and sufficient space to add in noodles or rice if appropriate.

If a recipe includes meat, always cut it into pieces across the grain to make it more tender. Marinating meat adds that extra depth of taste as well as tenderizing it. Keep your pieces the same size so they cook in the same length of time and are still easy to eat. Tofu should also be cut into cubes, and it is best marinated and fried before any final cooking as both processes help to increase the flavour and interest of a fairly bland product.

The recipes here are a real mixture of traditional flavours and contemporary tastes. By no means all of them contain meat because vegetables and fish are cheaper and more popular in Thailand and, of course, the majority of Thai people are vegetarian anyway. But any recipe should be flexible so it's up to you to experiment a little with the flavours and cooking styles. You will find that Thai curry pastes (see page 31), whether bought or home-made, will vary enormously in texture, colour and heat. Some recipes will ask for 2 tablespoons of curry paste, which you may find too hot, so if in doubt add it gradually and keep tasting as you cook. Basically, I would encourage you to cut up lots of fresh and colourful produce and stir-fry it quickly with zesty flavourings to make brilliant and mouthwatering dishes.

*Thai salads, like many other Thai dishes, are meant to be spicy and mouth-tingling*

# duck salad
## *yum ped*

1 Unwrap the duck and allow the skin to dry out overnight in the fridge.

2 The following day, slash the skin side 5 or 6 times. Mix the lemon grass, 2 tablespoons of the vegetable oil, all the sesame oil, fish sauce, chilli and curry paste together in a shallow dish and place the duck breasts in the mixture. Turn to coat and to rub the marinade into the meat. Chill for 2–3 hours.

3 Heat the remaining oil in a wok or large frying pan and fry the duck, skin side down, over a medium heat for 3–4 minutes until the skin is browned and crisp and the meat cooked most of the way through.

4 Turn the breasts over and fry until browned and the meat is cooked to your liking.

5 Meanwhile, arrange the pineapple, cucumber, tomatoes and onions on a platter. Mix the dressing ingredients together and pour over the top.

6 Lift the duck out of the wok and slice thickly. Arrange the duck slices on top of the salad and serve while still hot.

**SERVES 4**

4 boned duck breasts, skin on

1 lemon grass stalk, broken into three and each cut in half lengthways

3 tbsp vegetable or groundnut oil

2 tbsp sesame oil

1 tsp fish sauce

1 fresh green chilli, deseeded and chopped

2 tbsp Red Curry Paste (see page 31)

1/2 fresh pineapple, peeled and sliced*

7.5-cm/3-inch piece cucumber, peeled, deseeded and sliced

3 tomatoes, cut into wedges

1 onion, sliced thinly

*for the dressing*

juice of 1 lemon

2 garlic cloves, crushed

1 tsp palm sugar or soft, light brown sugar

2 tbsp vegetable or groundnut oil

*\*cook's tip*

You can reserve the pineapple leaves to use as a garnish.

202
# mixed seafood salad
*yum ta-le*

**SERVES 4**

3 tbsp vegetable or groundnut oil

1 small onion, sliced thinly

225 g/8 oz baby squid, cleaned and sliced

225 g/8 oz cooked prawns, peeled

500 g/1 lb mussels, unshelled

bunch of spring onions, chopped roughly

1 lemon grass stalk, chopped finely

1 red pepper, deseeded and cut into strips

1/2 small head Chinese leaves, shredded

2 garlic cloves, crushed

1 tsp fish sauce

1 tsp palm sugar or soft, light brown sugar

juice of 1 lemon

5-cm/2-inch piece cucumber, chopped

1 tomato, deseeded and chopped

1 Heat 1 tablespoon of the oil in a wok or large frying pan and stir-fry the onion, squid, prawns and mussels for 1–2 minutes, until the squid is opaque and the mussels have opened.

2 Mix the spring onions, lemon grass, red pepper and Chinese leaves together in a bowl. Add the seafood and stir gently. Turn into a serving dish.

3 Mix the garlic, the remaining oil, fish sauce, sugar, and lemon juice together. Add the chopped cucumber and tomato, spoon the dressing over the salad and seafood and serve immediately.

*Some Thai edifices are built on a vast scale*

# stir-fried vegetable salad
## *pahd puk*

**SERVES 4**

4 tbsp vegetable or groundnut oil

bunch of spring onions, chopped

$^1/_2$ small cabbage (any variety), shredded

225 g/8 oz fresh spinach, washed

225 g/8 oz pak choy, halved or quartered
  if necessary

175 g/6 oz Chinese or purple sprouting broccoli

1 small head Chinese leaves, shredded

few sprigs Thai basil

2 fresh red chillies, deseeded and chopped

2 tbsp oyster sauce

1 tsp palm sugar or soft, light brown sugar

1 tbsp sesame oil

2 tbsp sesame seeds, toasted

1 Heat 2 tablespoons of oil in a wok or large frying pan and fry the spring onions, all the leaves, basil and chillies quickly until just wilted. Transfer to a serving plate.

2 Mix the oyster sauce, sugar, the remaining vegetable oil and sesame oil together and pour over the leaves.

3 Scatter the sesame seeds over the top and serve immediately.

*Elegance is important to both architecture and cuisine*

206

# monkfish salad
## *yum pla*

**SERVES 4**

450 g/1 lb monkfish, skinned and boned

juice of 1 lime

3 tbsp vegetable or groundnut oil

1/2 tsp fish sauce

2 fresh red chillies, deseeded and sliced

75 g/3 oz plain flour

oil, for frying

1 Cos lettuce, torn into pieces

1/4 white cabbage, shredded

1 small onion, sliced thinly

*for the dressing*

juice of 1 lime

1 tsp palm sugar or soft, light brown sugar

1 tsp fish sauce

handful of fresh coriander, chopped

1 Cut the fish into even-sized cubes, each about 2.5 cm/1 inch and put into a shallow dish. Mix the lime juice, oil, fish sauce and chillies together and pour over the fish. Cover, chill and leave to marinate for 1–2 hours.

2 Put the flour onto a plate. Lift the fish out of the marinade and roll the pieces in the flour. Heat the oil in a wok or large frying pan and fry the fish, in batches if necessary, until browned all over. Lift out and drain on kitchen paper.

3 Put the lettuce, cabbage and onion on a serving platter and arrange the fish on top.

4 Mix the dressing ingredients together and pour over the whole salad. Serve immediately while the fish is still warm.

# tomato and squid salad
## *yum pla-muek*

**SERVES 4**

450 g/1 lb tomatoes

450 g/1 lb baby squid, cleaned and left whole

2 garlic cloves, chopped finely

2 fresh green chillies, deseeded and sliced

handful of fresh coriander, chopped

juice of 1 lime

1 tsp fish sauce

1 tbsp Thai soy sauce

1 Peel the tomatoes (see page 24). Cut into quarters, remove all the seeds and discard them. Finely chop the tomato flesh and set aside.

2 Bring a medium saucepan of water to the boil, add the squid and their tentacles and cook for 2–3 minutes. Remove and drain well.

3 Mix the tomatoes, garlic, chillies and half the coriander; add the squid and toss everything together. Turn into a serving dish.

4 Mix the lime juice, fish and soy sauces and the remaining coriander. Pour the dressing over the salad. Serve warm or cold.

*Sculpture and intricate decoration
are key elements of Thai art*

210 # crab and coriander salad
## *yum pue*

**SERVES 4**

350 g (12 oz) canned white crab meat, drained

4 spring onions, finely chopped

handful of fresh coriander, chopped

*for the dressing*

1 garlic clove, crushed

2.5-cm/1-inch piece root ginger, peeled and grated

2 lime leaves, torn into pieces

juice of 1 lime

1 tsp fish sauce

1 Webb's lettuce, shredded

7.5-cm/3-inch piece cucumber, chopped

1 Put the crab meat into a bowl and stir in the spring onions and coriander.

2 Mix the ingredients for the dressing together.

3 Place the lettuce leaves on a serving platter and scatter with the cucumber.

4 Arrange the crab salad over the leaves and drizzle the dressing over the salad. Serve immediately.

*Buddhist monks in their saffron-coloured robes are an integral part of society in Thailand*

# peppered beef salad
## *yum nuea*

SERVES 4

4 x 115 g/4 oz fillet steaks

2 tbsp black peppercorns, crushed

1 tsp Chinese five spice powder

115 g/4 oz beansprouts

2.5-cm/1-inch piece root ginger, chopped finely

4 shallots, sliced finely

1 red pepper, deseeded and sliced thinly

3 tbsp Thai soy sauce

2 fresh red chillies, deseeded and sliced

1/2 lemon grass stalk, chopped finely

3 tbsp vegetable or groundnut oil

1 tbsp sesame oil

1 Wash the steaks and pat dry on kitchen paper. Mix the peppercorns with the five spice and press onto all sides of the steaks. Cook on a griddle or under a grill for 2–3 minutes each side, or until cooked to your liking.

2 Meanwhile mix the beansprouts, half the ginger, the shallots and pepper together and share between 4 plates. Mix the remaining ginger, soy sauce, chillies, lemon grass and oils together.

3 Slice the beef and arrange on the vegetables. Drizzle with the dressing and serve immediately.

*Salad ingredients are bought daily in Thai markets*

214 # hot-and-sour vegetable salad
## *yum puk*

**SERVES 4**

2 tbsp vegetable or groundnut oil

1 tbsp chilli oil

1 onion, sliced

2.5-cm/1-inch piece root ginger, grated

1 small head broccoli, cut into florets

2 carrots, cut into matchsticks

1 red pepper, deseeded and cut into squares

1 yellow pepper, deseeded and cut into strips

50 g/2 oz mangetout, trimmed and halved

50 g/2 oz baby sweetcorn, halved

*for the dressing*

2 tbsp vegetable or groundnut oil

1 tsp chilli oil

1 tbsp rice wine vinegar

juice of 1 lime

1/2 tsp fish sauce

1 Heat the oils in a wok or large frying pan and fry the onion and ginger for 1–2 minutes until they start to soften. Add the vegetables and stir-fry for 2–3 minutes until they have softened slightly. Remove from the heat and set aside.

2 Mix the dressing ingredients together. Transfer the vegetables to a serving plate and drizzle the dressing over. Serve warm immediately, or allow the flavours to develop and serve cold.

*Right Thai families earn great merit when a son takes up the monk's robe*

*Overleaf Chillies are essential to many classic Thai dishes, and are used to flavour oil and dipping sauce*

# sea bass and mango salad
## *yum mamuang seabass*

**SERVES 2**

2 small sea bass, gutted and cleaned

1 tbsp Red Curry Paste (see page 31)

small handful of fresh coriander, chopped

150 ml/¹/₄ pint coconut milk

2 tbsp sweet chilli sauce

6–8 Thai basil leaves, chopped

¹/₂ tsp fish sauce

1 tsp rice wine vinegar

1 mango, stoned, peeled and sliced

selection of mixed salad leaves

1 Place the fish on a board. Mix the curry paste and coriander together and stuff inside each fish cavity. Cover and leave to marinate for 1–2 hours.

2 Preheat the oven to 200°C/400°F/Gas Mark 6. Place the fish in a roasting tin. Mix the coconut milk, chilli sauce, basil, fish sauce, and vinegar and pour over the fish. Arrange the mango slices in the tin as well. Cover with foil and cook for 15 minutes.

3 Remove the foil and cook uncovered for a further 10–15 minutes until cooked.

4 Place the fish on 2 warmed serving plates, drizzle with the cooking sauces and serve with the mixed salad leaves.

*An abundance of fresh fish is available in Thailand's markets*

220 # red chicken salad
*yum ped daeng*

**SERVES 4**

4 boned chicken breasts

2 tbsp Red Curry Paste (see page 31)

2 tbsp vegetable or groundnut oil

1 head Chinese leaves, shredded

175 g/6 oz pak choy, torn into large pieces

1/2 Savoy cabbage, shredded

2 shallots, chopped finely

2 garlic cloves, crushed

1 tbsp rice wine vinegar

2 tbsp sweet chilli sauce

2 tbsp Thai soy sauce

1 Slash the flesh of the chicken several times and rub the curry paste into each cut. Cover and chill overnight.

2 Cook in a heavy-based saucepan over a medium heat or on a griddle for 5-6 minutes, turning once or twice, until cooked through. Keep warm.

3 Heat 1 tablespoon of the oil in a wok or large frying pan and stir-fry the leaves, pak choy and cabbage until just wilted. Add the remaining oil, shallots and garlic and stir-fry until just tender but not browned. Add the vinegar, chilli sauce and soy. Remove from the heat.

4 Arrange the leaves on 4 serving plates. Slice the chicken, arrange on the salad leaves and drizzle the hot dressing over. Serve immediately.

*Lemon grass is a popular ingredient that adds a distinctive flavour to salads, soups and sauces*

# prawn and pawpaw salad
## *somtam gung*

**SERVES 4**

1 pawpaw, peeled

350 g/12 oz large cooked prawns, shelled

*for the dressing*

4 spring onions, chopped finely

2 fresh red chillies, deseeded and chopped finely

1 tsp fish sauce

1 tbsp vegetable or groundnut oil

juice of 1 lime

1 tsp palm sugar or soft, light brown sugar

assorted baby green salad leaves

1 Scoop the seeds out of the pawpaw and slice thinly. Stir gently together with the prawns.

2 Mix the spring onions, chillies, fish sauce, oil, lime juice and sugar together.

3 Arrange the salad leaves in a bowl and top with the pawpaw and prawns. Pour the dressing over and serve immediately.

*A trip to a Thai market can provide a friendly discussion and an array of salad items*

224

# curried egg salad
## *yum khai*

**SERVES 4**

6 eggs

1 tbsp vegetable or groundnut oil

1 onion, chopped

1 tbsp Yellow Curry Paste (see page 93)

4 tbsp natural yogurt

1/2 tsp salt

handful of fresh coriander, chopped finely

bunch of watercress

2 courgettes, cut into matchsticks

1 fresh green chilli, deseeded and chopped finely

1 tsp fish sauce

1 tsp rice wine vinegar

3 tbsp vegetable or groundnut oil

1 Put the eggs in a saucepan, cover with cold water and bring to the boil. Simmer for 10 minutes, then drain and rinse in cold water. Shell and halve.

2 Meanwhile, heat the oil in a medium frying pan and fry the onion gently until softened but not browned. Remove from the heat and stir in the curry paste. Cool slightly before stirring in the yogurt, salt and half the coriander. Set aside.

3 Arrange the watercress and courgettes on a platter. Mix the chilli, fish sauce, vinegar and oil together and pour the dressing over the leaves.

4 Arrange the eggs on top and spoon the yogurt mixture over each one. Garnish with the remaining coriander over the top and serve immediately.

# gingered chicken and vegetable salad

## *yum gai khing*

**SERVES 4**

4 skinned, boned chicken breasts

4 spring onions, chopped

2.5-cm/1-inch piece root ginger, chopped finely

2 garlic cloves, crushed

2 tbsp vegetable or groundnut oil

*for the salad*

1 tbsp vegetable or groundnut oil

1 onion, sliced

2 garlic cloves, chopped

115 g/4 oz baby sweetcorn, halved

115 g/4 oz mangetout, halved lengthways

1 red pepper, deseeded and sliced

7.5-cm/3-inch piece cucumber, peeled,
  deseeded and sliced

4 tbsp Thai soy sauce

1 tbsp palm sugar or soft, light brown sugar

few Thai basil leaves

175 g/6 oz fine egg noodles

1 Cut the chicken into large cubes, each about 2.5 cm/ 1 inch. Mix the spring onions, ginger, garlic and oil together in a shallow dish and add the chicken. Cover and marinate for at least 3 hours. Lift the meat out of the marinade and set aside.

2 Heat the oil in a wok or large frying pan and fry the onion for 1–2 minutes before adding the rest of the vegetables except the cucumber. Fry for 2–3 minutes, until just tender. Add the cucumber, half the soy sauce, the sugar and basil and mix gently.

3 Soak the noodles for 2–3 minutes (check the packet instructions) or until tender and drain well. Sprinkle the remaining soy sauce over them and arrange on plates. Top with the cooked vegetables.

4 Add a little more oil to the wok if necessary and fry the chicken over a fairly high heat until browned on all sides. Arrange the chicken cubes on top of the salad and serve hot or warm.

# julienne vegetable salad
*yum puk foi*

**SERVES 4**

4 tbsp vegetable or groundnut oil

225 g/8 oz tofu with herbs, cubed

1 red onion, sliced

4 spring onions, cut into 5-cm/2-inch lengths

1 garlic clove, chopped

2 carrots, cut into matchsticks

115 g/4 oz fine French beans, trimmed

1 yellow pepper, deseeded and cut into strips

115 g/4 oz broccoli, cut into florets

1 large courgette, cut into matchsticks

50 g/2 oz beansprouts

2 tbsp Red Curry Paste (see page 31)

4 tbsp Thai soy sauce

1 tbsp rice wine vinegar

1 tsp palm sugar or soft, light brown sugar

few Thai basil leaves

350 g/12 oz rice vermicelli noodles

1 Heat the oil in a wok or large frying pan and fry the tofu cubes for 3–4 minutes, until browned on all sides. Lift out of the oil and drain on kitchen paper.

2 Add the onions, garlic and carrots to the hot oil and fry for 1–2 minutes before adding the rest of the vegetables, except for the beansprouts. Stir-fry for 2–3 minutes. Add the beansprouts, then stir in the curry paste, soy, vinegar, sugar and basil leaves. Cook for 30 seconds.

3 Soak the noodles in boiling water or stock for 2–3 minutes (check the packet instructions) or until tender and drain well.

4 Pile the vegetables onto the noodles, and serve topped with the tofu cubes. Garnish with extra basil if liked.

# aubergine and onion salad
## *yum makuea*

*This looks attractive made with an assortment of aubergine varieties. No matter what you use, make sure they are all cut to the same size.*

SERVES 4

4 tbsp vegetable or groundnut oil

1 onion, sliced

4 shallots, chopped finely

4 spring onions, sliced

350 g/12 oz aubergines, cubed

2 tbsp Green Curry Paste (see page 31)

2 tbsp Thai soy sauce

1 tsp palm sugar or soft, light brown sugar

115 g/4 oz creamed coconut, chopped

3 tbsp water

small handful of fresh coriander, chopped

few Thai basil leaves, chopped

small handful of fresh parsley, chopped

115 g/4 oz rocket leaves

2 tbsp sweet chilli sauce

1 Heat half the oil in a wok or large frying pan and fry all the onions together for 1–2 minutes, until just softened but not browned. Lift out and reserve.

2 Fry the aubergine cubes, in batches if necessary, adding more oil as necessary, until they are crisp and golden brown.

3 Return the onions to the wok and add the curry paste, soy sauce and sugar. Add the creamed coconut and water and cook until dissolved. Stir in most of the coriander, the basil and parsley.

4 Toss the rocket in the chilli sauce and serve with the aubergine and onion salad. Garnish with the remaining herbs.

# DESSERTS

This last section of the book is a bit of a cheat. Thai people don't really eat the same sort of desserts at home as we do in the West. They might have fresh fruit or tapioca, or dumplings made from mung bean flour, but having no dairy products means no cream, chocolate, or cheesecakes. This might sound disappointing to sweet-toothed people, but it needn't be.

I know people who look at the dessert menu first, decide how much space they need to leave for their pudding and adjust their other courses accordingly. So I had to find a way around this potential drawback to the Thai menu. Dumplings with red bean jam in the centre may not appeal to many Western palates – we tend to want something sweeter and more familiar and need to find ways to combine Thailand's produce to make everyone happy. It's actually turned out to be very easy, as the flavours, spices and fruit of the country lend themselves to lots of different desserts that we in the West can instantly recognize.

After all the exciting, spicy flavours of one or two first courses, our taste buds may well need something to calm them down. So I have majored on those desserts which combine some of the wonderful fruit and nuts that are sold in colourful abundance in the markets in Thailand with some of the sweeter spices to complete the Thai experience.

You don't need any specialist equipment, just a whisk, ramekins and the usual range of saucepans and frying pans. There is an ice cream recipe, as well as one for a pineapple and lime sorbet, so if you have an ice cream maker, these desserts would be ideal and straightforward to prepare. However, as I suspect most of us don't have one of these machines, these two freezer desserts will have to be made in the more traditional way.

Thailand produces coconuts, pineapples and bananas, and the more exotic lychees and pomelos. These fruits are varied in flavour and texture – and deliciously versatile. Bananas can be mashed, or barbecued, or sliced into salads. (Toss them in lime or lemon juice once peeled, as they discolour quickly.) The easiest way to peel a pineapple is to cut off the leafy top and base, cut it into thick slices and then trim away the tough skin with a sharp knife. If the fruit is ripe, the core will be soft enough to eat; if not, cut it out and discard. If you want to use fresh coconut, here's a good way to open it. Use a hammer to tap around the centre of the shell. Keep tapping and turning and eventually the shell will crack in half. (Hold it over a bowl while you do this to catch the liquid once the nut cracks open.)

## the flavours, spices and fruit ... lend themselves to lots of different desserts that we ... can recognize

I have used spices, such as ginger and cinnamon, in combination with these fruits to make the best use of Thailand's great flavours. Ground ginger and cinnamon are widely available. Balls of preserved stem ginger covered with syrup can be chopped into ice creams or cakes, or sliced and used to decorate creamy desserts and fools. Cinnamon sticks added to simmering milk provide extra flavour (discard them before serving or freezing). Both of these should be available in supermarkets, grocers or delicatessens.

You will never find this type of dessert in Thailand or a Thai restaurant, as Thais simply do not eat this type of food. These recipes have been created to combine the traditional flavours of this beautiful country with Western contemporary expectations of what makes a good dessert.

236

# banana and coconut ice cream
## *i tim ma-prown sai khuay*

**SERVES 6–8**

85 g/3 oz creamed coconut, chopped

600 ml/1 pint double cream

225 g/8 oz icing sugar

2 bananas

1 tsp lemon juice

fresh fruit, to serve

1 Put the creamed coconut in a small bowl. Add just enough boiling water to cover and stir until dissolved. Leave to cool.

2 Whip the cream with the icing sugar until thick but still floppy.* Mash the bananas with the lemon juice and whisk gently into the cream together with the cold coconut.

3 Transfer to a freezerproof container and freeze overnight. Serve in scoops with fresh fruit.

*cook's tip
Take care not to overwhip the cream or it will curdle when the other ingredients are added.

*The highly prized lotus flower*

# creamy mango brûlée
## *mamuang*

1 Slice the mangoes on either side of the stone. Discard the stone and peel the fruit. Slice and then chop the fruit. Divide it between 4 ramekins.

2 Beat the mascarpone cheese with the yogurt. Fold in the ginger, lime rind and juice and soft brown sugar. Divide the mixture between the ramekins and level off the tops. Chill for 2 hours.

3 Sprinkle 2 tablespoons of demerara sugar over the top of each dish, covering the creamy mixture. Place under a hot grill for 2–3 minutes, until melted and browned. Cool, then chill until required.
This dessert should be eaten on the day of making.

**SERVES 4**

**2 mangoes**

**250 g/9 oz mascarpone cheese**

**200 ml/7 fl oz Greek-style yogurt**

**1 tsp ground ginger**

**grated rind and juice of 1 lime**

**2 tbsp soft, light brown sugar**

**8 tbsp demerara sugar**

*Some of the images of Buddha are made of solid gold*

240 spicy rice pudding
*kau mun*

1 Put the coconut milk and milk in a saucepan and heat gently. Add the sugar and stir until it has dissolved.

2 Add the rice and spice and gradually bring to the boil. Simmer gently, stirring frequently, for 45–60 minutes, until thickened.

3 Stir in the butter and once it has melted, serve immediately, sprinkled with cinnamon.

**SERVES 4**

**400 ml/14 fl oz canned coconut milk**

**150 ml/1/4 pint milk**

**55 g/2 oz soft brown sugar**

**55 g/2 oz pudding rice**

**2 tsp mixed spice**

**25 g/1 oz butter**

**1 tsp ground cinnamon**

*The rivers and canals of the central plain are its peaceful highways*

# pineapple and lime sorbet 243
## *subparot, ma-nau i tim*

SERVES 4

225 g/8 oz caster sugar

600 ml/1 pint water

grated rind and juice of 2 limes

1 small pineapple, peeled, quartered and chopped*

sweet biscuits, to serve

*\*cook's tip*
You can also halve the pineapple, cut out the flesh, and use the shell as an attractive way of serving the sorbet.

1 Put the sugar and water into a saucepan and heat gently, stirring until the sugar has dissolved. Bring to the boil and simmer for 10 minutes.

2 Stir in the grated rind and half the lime juice. Remove from the heat and leave to cool.

3 Put the pineapple in a blender or food processor and process until smooth. Add to the cold syrup with the remaining lime juice. Pour into a freezerproof container and freeze until crystals have formed around the edge.

4 Turn out the sorbet into a bowl. Beat well with a fork to break up the crystals. Return to the freezer and chill overnight. Serve in scoops with sweet biscuits.

*The night sky in Thailand is lit up with the distinctive shapes of its shrines and temples*

244

# mixed fruit salad
## *polamai ruam*

**SERVES 4**

1 pawpaw, halved, peeled and deseeded

2 bananas, sliced thickly

1 small pineapple, peeled, halved, cored and sliced

12 lychees, peeled

1 small melon, deseeded and cut into thin wedges

2 oranges

grated rind and juice of 1 lime

2 tbsp caster sugar

1 Arrange the pawpaw, bananas, pineapple, lychees and melon on a serving platter. Cut off the rind and pith from the oranges. Cut the orange slices out from between the membranes and add to the fruit platter.

2 Combine the lime rind, juice and sugar. Pour over the salad and serve.

**SERVES 4**

55 g/2 oz creamed coconut, chopped

150 ml/¼ pint boiling water

225 g/8 oz plain flour

2 tbsp caster sugar

2 eggs

450 ml/¾ pint milk

25 g/1 oz desiccated coconut

55 g/2 oz butter

½ melon, deseeded, peeled and sliced thinly

1 Put the creamed coconut in a bowl, pour in the measured water and stir until dissolved.

2 Sift the flour in another bowl and stir in the sugar. Beat in the eggs and half the milk. Gradually beat in the remaining milk and then the coconut mixture to make a creamy batter. Stir in the desiccated coconut.

3 Melt a little of the butter in a heavy-based frying pan. Add 3–4 tablespoons of the batter, spacing them well apart as they will spread during cooking. Cook for 1–2 minutes, then flip over to cook the second side. Remove from the frying pan and keep warm. Cook the remaining batter in the same way. Serve warm with melon slices.

*Overleaf Shrines and temples are sometimes in isolated or wooded areas. Treat any sacred place with great respect*

248

# banana-stuffed crêpes
## *pang ho khuay*

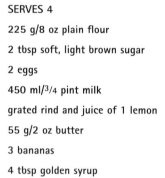

SERVES 4

225 g/8 oz plain flour

2 tbsp soft, light brown sugar

2 eggs

450 ml/3/4 pint milk

grated rind and juice of 1 lemon

55 g/2 oz butter

3 bananas

4 tbsp golden syrup

1 Combine the flour and sugar and beat in the eggs and half the milk. Beat together until smooth. Gradually add the remaining milk, stirring constantly to make a smooth batter. Stir in the lemon rind.

2 Melt a little butter in a 20-cm/8-inch frying pan and pour in a quarter of the batter. Tilt the frying pan to coat the base and cook for 1–2 minutes, until set. Flip the crêpe over and cook the second side. Slide out of the frying pan and keep warm. Repeat to make 3 more pancakes.

3 Slice the bananas and toss in the lemon juice. Pour the syrup over them and toss together. Fold each pancake into 4 and fill the centre with the banana mixture. Serve warm.

*A close-up of the ornamental decoration on a roof support*

250

# roasted spicy pineapple
## *subparot ob*

**SERVES 4**

1 pineapple

1 mango, peeled, stoned and sliced

55 g/2 oz butter

4 tbsp golden syrup

1–2 tsp cinnamon

1 tsp freshly grated nutmeg

4 tbsp soft brown sugar

2 passion fruit

150 ml/¼ pint soured cream

finely grated rind of 1 orange

1 Preheat the oven to 200°C/400°F/Gas Mark 6. Use a sharp knife to cut off the top, base and skin of the pineapple, then cut into quarters. Remove the central core and cut the flesh into large cubes. Place them in a roasting tin with the mango.

2 Place the butter, syrup, cinnamon, nutmeg and sugar in a small saucepan and heat gently, stirring constantly, until melted. Pour the mixture over the fruit. Roast for 20–30 minutes, until the fruit is browned.

3 Halve the passion fruit and scoop out the seeds. Spoon over the roasted fruit. Mix the soured cream and orange rind together and serve with the fruit.

1 Put the creamed coconut and cream in a small saucepan and heat gently until the coconut has dissolved. Remove from the heat and set aside to cool for 10 minutes, then whisk until thick but floppy.

2 Peel the bananas and toss in the lime juice and rind. Lightly oil a preheated griddle pan and cook the bananas, turning once, for 2–3 minutes, until soft and browned.

3 Toast the desiccated coconut on a piece of foil under a grill until lightly browned. Serve the bananas with the coconut cream, sprinkled with the toasted coconut.

# griddled bananas
## *khuay ping*

**SERVES 4**

**55 g/2 oz creamed coconut, chopped**

**150 ml/$^1$/$_4$ pint double cream**

**4 bananas**

**juice and rind of 1 lime**

**1 tbsp vegetable or groundnut oil**

**50 g/1$^3$/$_4$ oz desiccated coconut**

252

# ginger creams and sesame pastries
*ka-num rung ob yha rad na khing*

1 Whip the cream until thick, but not floppy. Stir in the yogurt and the ginger syrup. Divide the stem ginger between 4 glasses or cups and then top with the ginger cream. Sprinkle 1 tablespoon of sugar on each one and chill overnight.

2 Preheat the oven to 200°C/400°F/Gas Mark 6. Cut the filo pastry into 16 x 10-cm/4-inch squares. Brush 1 square with melted butter, then place another square on top. Repeat twice more to make a 4-layered pastry. Make 3 more in the same way.

3 Brush with butter and sprinkle with sesame seeds and bake for 10–15 minutes, until golden brown. Serve warm with the ginger creams.

**SERVES 4**

450 ml/³/₄ pint double cream

150 ml/¹/₄ pint natural yogurt

4 tbsp ginger syrup (from the stem ginger jar)

6 pieces preserved stem ginger, chopped

4 tbsp soft brown sugar

115 g/4 oz filo pastry

55 g/2 oz butter, melted

3 tbsp sesame seeds

*Thailand boasts paradise beaches as well as vibrant cities*

## 254 index